Union veterans of the Maryland Department, Grand Army of the Republic, parade through Boston on August 21, 1917, during the organization's 51st National Encampment. In 1915, the nation had marked the 50th anniversary of the end of the Civil War. Memories of Maryland's bitter Civil War divisions still lingered, but the Maryland National Guard that mobilized for war in 1917 boasted lineages from both Union and Confederate units. (Author's collection.)

ON THE COVER: Exuberant and weary soldiers of "Maryland's Own" 115th Infantry Regiment and the 112th Machine Gun Battalion return to the United States aboard the transport USS *Artemis* in 1919. Both units were part of the 29th "Blue and Gray" Division, National Guard, and together sustained a casualty rate of nearly 28 percent during the war, including 207 killed and 799 wounded. (Author's collection.)

IMAGES
of America

MARYLAND IN
WORLD WAR I

William M. Armstrong

ARCADIA
PUBLISHING

Published by Arcadia Publishing
Charleston, South Carolina

Library of Congress Control Number: 2016958166

For all general information, please contact Arcadia Publishing:
Telephone 843-853-2070
Fax 843-853-0044
E-mail sales@arcadiapublishing.com
For customer service and orders:
Toll-Free 1-888-313-2665

Visit us on the Internet at www.arcadiapublishing.com

*Dedicated to Elizabeth, Riley, and Joshua,
and in memory of Patricia Cadigan Armstrong;
Pfc. L. Raymond DuRoss, American Expeditionary Forces;
and Pte. James Tapp, Canadian Expeditionary Force.*

CONTENTS

ACKNOWLEDGMENTS

This book would not have been possible without the generous contributions of many individuals, starting with the men and women who served and sacrificed at the nation's behest, the photographers and other journalists who documented their service, and the various organizations and individuals who have preserved the historical record.

I would like to especially thank my friend Paul Cora, curator at Historic Ships in Baltimore and chair of the Western Front Association East Coast Branch (USA); Jonathan Eaker of the Library of Congress; Joseph Balkoski at the Maryland Museum of Military History; Elizabeth Novara, Eric Stoykovich, and Anne Turkos of the University of Maryland; Sen. Joseph D. Tydings; Ned, Preston, and Stanhope Goddard; Gregory Weidman and ranger Paul Plamann of the National Park Service, Fort McHenry National Monument and Historic Shrine; Lisa Marine of the Wisconsin Historical Society; Patrizia Nava, Thomas Allen, and Paul Oelkrug at the Eugene McDermott Library, the University of Texas at Dallas; Shawn Gladden of the Howard County Historical Society; Kathy Lafferty of the Spencer Research Library, University of Kansas; Sarah Windham of Stanley Black & Decker; Pat Andersen of the Montgomery County Historical Society; the staff of the Harvard University Archives; and the staff of the Still Pictures Branch of the National Archives and Records Administration, College Park, Maryland. I would also like to give special thanks to my amazing wife, Elizabeth, who has provided valuable advice and feedback throughout the development of this book, and my son, Joshua, and daughter, Riley, for being an inspiration and for their patience as I sort through (in four-year-old Joshua's words) "pictures that are old." I hope that I have done your efforts justice.

The majority of the photographs in this book were obtained from the Still Pictures and Textual Branches of the National Archives and Records Administration (NARA), College Park, Maryland; the Prints and Photographs Division of the Library of Congress (LOC); and the US Navy's Naval History and Heritage Command (NHHC). The image of Theodore Roosevelt is from the Theodore Roosevelt Birthplace National Historic Site Collection at the Theodore Roosevelt Digital Library, Dickinson State University.

INTRODUCTION

"Austrian Heir and Wife Slain:" the news made the *Baltimore Sun's* front page on Monday, June 29, 1914. The paper covered the tragedy in considerable detail, though its ultimate consequences could not be predicted. The previous day, in the Bosnian city of Sarajevo (then part of Austria-Hungary), a group of ethnic Serbian separatists had set out to assassinate visiting Archduke Franz Ferdinand, heir to the Austro-Hungarian throne. The plot had nearly failed, but then a wrong turn placed the archduke's car within feet of conspirator Gavrilo Princip. The Bosnian Serb seized his opportunity, fatally shooting the archduke and his wife before being subdued. Ethnic tensions in the region erupted, and Austria-Hungary used the assassination to justify invading neighboring Serbia.

Thus was triggered a network of military alliances, as Russia committed to Serbia's defense. Germany allied with Austria-Hungary, as well as the Ottoman Empire. Britain and France ultimately sided with Russia, and were eventually joined by Italy. Colonial possessions were dragged into the fight, and other nations, less directly involved, soon joined.

German forces had struck toward Paris in August, sweeping through Luxembourg and Belgium en route. Despite initial success, the German advance into France was soon halted, and over the next several years, a relatively static war took place along the trenches of the western front. Meanwhile, fighting continued along the eastern front with Russia and in Southern Europe, the Middle East, Africa, and East Asia, as well as at sea. The United States remained officially neutral and enjoyed the resultant prosperity, and Maryland was no exception. The nation had its own, albeit minor, military operations to manage, in Mexico and along its border, escalated by the Battle of Veracruz in April 1914. Official neutrality, however, did not keep Americans from taking sides.

The preponderance of American support was for Britain and France, widely regarded as defenders of democracy against totalitarianism and barbarism, and a number of Americans (including Marylanders) even went to fight on their behalf. Many other Americans had a financial stake in Allied victory: American investors helped bankroll the Allied war effort, while American firms (and the overall economy) profited from Allied war contracts. Loud voices, including that of former president Theodore Roosevelt, called for the United States to join the Allies outright and send troops to the western front.

Yet not everyone saw Germany as a villainous threat. In a war generally characterized by nationalism more than ideology, many sided with the countries of their ancestry or simply refused to side with their opponents. Initially, that included many members of the large German American community in Maryland and across the nation. In addition, for a variety of reasons, a sizable portion of the general population remained indifferent or outright isolationist.

The war gradually found its way to the United States. In 1915, people around the world, not least Americans, were appalled when a German submarine deliberately sank the British luxury liner RMS *Lusitania*. Combined with longstanding awareness of German atrocities, particularly against Belgian civilians, that were played up for Allied propaganda purposes but rooted in grim reality, the sinking seemingly gave credence to the propaganda image of Germans as the dastardly "Hun." Germany was also well aware of America's material support for the Allies, and its saboteurs and spies prowled the country, aided by German American sympathizers, sowing labor discord and carrying out acts of violent sabotage. Only a few were ever caught, but paranoia and xenophobia spread.

In the face of these events, Pres. Woodrow Wilson's administration went to great lengths to assure the wary public that America was "too proud to fight" yet prepared for whatever might come. Despite the strength of pro-Allied sentiment, the majority of the country remained stoutly opposed to taking up arms, and Wilson's 1916 reelection campaign famously used the slogan "He Has Kept Us Out Of War." But events the following year would erode public patience.

By 1917, Germany was in peril. While the European land war was largely a stalemate, Britain's naval blockade left the country nearly starving and short of vital war materiel. Desperate to regain the upper hand, Germany made the decision to resume unrestricted submarine warfare against Allied merchant ships, a policy that had been abandoned to appease the United States after the *Lusitania* disaster. The decision was controversial, even in Germany, due to fear that the United States would finally be pushed into war.

Soon German submarines were sinking American ships and killing more American citizens. Then came German foreign secretary Arthur Zimmermann's infamous telegram to the German ambassador to Mexico in early 1917, a clumsy and ill-advised attempt to forge an alliance with Mexico against the United States. British intelligence intercepted and deciphered the document and turned it over to the US State Department. Wilson asked for a declaration of war on April 2, 1917, which Congress delivered on April 6. Maryland's congressional delegation unanimously supported the declaration (Sen. John Walter Smith did not vote, having left the Capitol due to a family death). Yet when war finally came, the United States was still largely unprepared—a factor of singular importance in examining the American war effort.

The first Maryland troops arrived overseas in time to help blunt the Germans' last, desperate offensives in the spring and summer of 1918. Motivated by Russia's exit from the war, which freed soldiers from the eastern front, as well as by the impending arrival of American forces, Germany made significant gains but fell short of any strategic victory. The bulk of Maryland's troops, in the National Guard and National Army, arrived in time for what became the Allies' last western front offensives in September 1918. They participated in the Meuse-Argonne Offensive, a joint French and American operation that began on September 26, 1918, and lasted until the Armistice of November 11. The speed with which Germany collapsed during the final Allied onslaught was unexpected. Maryland units were among those preparing for further assaults. Many American troops in France never reached the front, and many more never even crossed the Atlantic.

This is a history of Maryland's role as the United States rose to the challenge of fighting its first global war. As a photographic history, it is by nature incomplete. We are fortunate to have such a rich photographic record of those times, but of course photographers did not capture everything. Many photographs were taken for propaganda purposes and avoided the darker aspects of wartime history. For instance, in this book you will see very little of the war's horrors. The segregation and prevailing racial attitudes of the time helped ensure that relatively little photographic coverage was given to African Americans during the war, although they made up nearly 17 percent of Maryland's wartime population. Women, too, received scant coverage disproportionate to their efforts. Notable controversies and civil unrest often evaded photographic documentation. Much of the time, frontline operations evaded photographers as well—photographs showing soldiers in actual combat were rare, due to both the difficulty of taking combat photographs in general and the limitations of the era's camera equipment. Yet these photographs, most never before published, provide a valuable glimpse into Marylanders' wartime experiences, which to a large degree reflected the experiences of all Americans.

One

NEUTRALITY

Within 10 years, Baltimore had risen from the ashes of the Great Fire, which gutted much of the downtown area in 1904, emerging vibrant and more modern. Still, city life presented images both old and new: horse-drawn carts and paddle steamers, automobiles and ocean liners. Not until 1918 would the city complete its geographic expansion, annexing parts of Anne Arundel and Baltimore Counties. (LOC.)

Baltimore loved parades, and there was no better excuse than the 100th anniversary of "The Star-Spangled Banner." Maryland lawyer Francis Scott Key's poem was inspired by the defense of Fort McHenry during British bombardment the night of September 13–14, 1814. The popular song would later become the national anthem. Throughout the weeklong centennial celebration, the First Battle of the Marne raged in France, resulting in over 500,000 casualties. (Author's collection.)

The 1854 sloop-of-war USS *Constellation* arrives at the mouth of the Jones Falls in Baltimore Harbor during the Star-Spangled Banner Centennial festivities. The patriotic extravaganza lasted from September 6 to 13, with representatives from every state in attendance. Then based in Newport, Rhode Island, the *Constellation* would later train US Navy personnel headed off to the "Great War." Today it is an iconic museum ship in Baltimore's Inner Harbor. (NHHC.)

The *Lusitania* enters New York Harbor. The German submarine *U-20* torpedoed the famous British luxury liner just 11 miles off the coast of Ireland on May 5, 1915. The *Lusitania* sank quickly, killing 1,198, including 128 Americans. Although the *Lusitania* was carrying munitions, and Germany had warned passengers not to embark on the voyage, the sinking caused international outrage and helped turn American public opinion against Germany. (NARA.)

Pallbearers carry a victim of the *Lusitania* through Queenstown (now Cobh), Ireland. Maryland's dead included Henry Sonneborn and his partner, Leo Schwabacher, and siblings Elaine and Charles Harwood Knight. All were Baltimore natives except Schwabacher, who was originally from Illinois. The local press reserved most coverage for prominent New York multimillionaire Alfred Vanderbilt, whose Baltimorean widow, Margaret Emerson, was heir to the Bromo-Seltzer fortune. Their bodies were never recovered. (LOC.)

Kapitänleutnant Paul König of the German merchant submarine *Deutschland* arrives off Baltimore in July 1916, greeted by Baltimore native Paul Hilken (far right). König successfully evaded Britain's naval blockade to reach America, capturing the world's attention. He was welcomed by Mayor James Preston and greeted as a celebrity by many Baltimoreans. Hilken, a prominent businessman, represented the North German Lloyd Shipping Company, the *Deutschland's* nominal operator. (LOC.)

The *Deutschland* brought scarce, high-quality German dye, which sold for over $6 million (a profit of over 2,900 percent). When the submarine departed Baltimore on August 2, it carried nearly 877 tons of cargo, mostly nickel and crude rubber essential to the German war effort. Yet the cargo U-boat concept quickly proved too inefficient, and in 1917, the German navy converted the *Deutschland* into the armed *U-155*. (LOC.)

FOR THE BENEFIT OF THE
PRISONERS OF WAR IN SIBERIA

IN COMMEMORATION OF THE FIRST TRANSATLANTIC VOYAGE OF THE SUBMARINE LINER
"DEUTSCHLAND" BALTIMORE, MD. JULY 9TH 1916.

One of many postcards commemorating the *Deutschland*'s Maryland visit, this design was printed on behalf of a New York–based charity. The *Deutschland* later made a second voyage, to Connecticut, but that visit was clouded by controversy. By then, many suspected that the *Deutschland* was secretly operated by the German government and crewed by naval personnel, which it was—most remained with the vessel after it became the *U-155*. (LOC.)

Hansa Haus, at the corner of Charles and German Streets in Baltimore, was home to both the German consulate and the North German Lloyd Shipping Company (whose ships brought many immigrants). From here, Paul Hilken oversaw and financed a loose network of saboteurs on behalf of the German government, including biological warfare operatives who produced anthrax and glanders at a secret laboratory in Chevy Chase. (Courtesy of the Maryland Historical Society.)

13

On July 30, 1916, explosions obliterated the Black Tom depot in New Jersey, where munitions purchased by the Allies awaited shipment. Even some Marylanders felt the blasts, which killed seven and injured hundreds. The sabotage network orchestrated by Paul Hilken was responsible for this and other German sabotage operations in the United States. Hilken revealed his group's role years later, after being granted immunity to testify. (LOC.)

Gen. Francisco "Pancho" Villa (center right), seething after the United States switched alliance to his rivals during the Mexican Revolution, conducted a series of deadly cross-border supply raids. At Columbus, New Mexico, his force killed 18 Americans. The March 1916 Mexican Expedition to capture Villa, led by Brig. Gen. John Pershing, provided limited combat experience for some soldiers. Pershing would soon command the American Expeditionary Forces (AEF) in France. (LOC.)

Company H, 5th Maryland Infantry Regiment, encamped at Eagle Pass, Texas. While only Regular Army personnel participated in the "Punitive Expedition" against Villa in Mexico, many National Guard units were mobilized for Border War service in 1916–1917. Maryland sent three infantry regiments, cavalry, and medical units. Continuing deadly border raids by various Mexican factions, met with American military reprisals, severely strained US-Mexican relations. (Courtesy of the Maryland Museum of Military History.)

Riflemen of Company H look the part in the Texas desert. They are equipped with the M1903 Springfield rifle, which would serve in both world wars. Texas weather was the most formidable adversary that the Maryland National Guard encountered, but the experience provided valuable training. Kneeling at center is Pvt. Henry G. Costin, who would later earn the Medal of Honor in France. (Courtesy of the Maryland Museum of Military History.)

Above, soldiers of Company H, 5th Maryland Infantry, guard the International Bridge over the Rio Grande at Eagle Pass. The machine gunners below are operating an American M1909 version of the French Hotchkiss Benét–Mercié. The 4th and 1st Maryland Infantry were the first to return from border service, in September and November 1916, respectively. In March 1917, they began performing similar duties along the Susquehanna and Potomac Rivers, guarding bridges against possible German sabotage. Detachments also guarded railroad tunnels, munitions plants, and Baltimore's water supplies at Lake Montebello and Loch Raven. The 5th Maryland returned from Texas and mustered out in February 1917, with elements joining the other two infantry regiments on guard duty on the day before Congress declared war on Germany. (Both, courtesy of the Maryland Museum of Military History.)

Two

MARYLAND'S HOME FRONT

During the war, the Hochschild, Kohn and Company department store at 201 Howard Street in Baltimore was adorned with this US Food Administration sign urging citizens to conserve food for the war effort. In December 1917, the store began selling a 25¢ *Conservation Cook Book*, with recipes covering "everything from wheatless breads to sugarless candies." The company employed about 1,500 during the war. (NARA.)

Proud volunteers pose at Salisbury's Community Garden, the first in Wicomico County. The Maryland Council of Defense, in cooperation with the Maryland State College of Agriculture (now University of Maryland, College Park), actively encouraged communities to rely on war gardens for their food supply, enabling commercial farms to devote themselves to war work. (NARA.)

These women were members of Salisbury's Canning Club, which was part of a nationwide effort to preserve home- and community-grown food. Their goal was to reduce spoilage and free commercial canning firms for war contracts in order to feed the rapidly expanding military and America's war-ravaged allies. In Maryland, a number of local canning groups operated under the Women's Section of the Council of Defense. (NARA.)

Members of the Potomac Unit of the Woman's Land Army of the District of Columbia work a farm in Montgomery County. The Woman's Land Army, modeled after the similarly named organization in Britain, trained farmhands to take the place of men inducted into the military. Dubbed "Farmerettes" by the press, they helped ease a critical farm labor shortage beginning in the spring of 1918, winning high praise from local farmers. Many of the women were college students or teachers. While the Potomac Unit worked farms in Montgomery and Prince George's Counties, the separate Woman's Land Army of Maryland operated camps across other parts of the state under the Food Production Committee of the Women's Section, Maryland Council of Defense. (Both, courtesy of the Montgomery County Historical Society.)

French marshal Joseph Joffre helps break ground for the Lafayette Monument in Mount Vernon on May 14, 1917, as Mayor Preston (second from left) and other officials look on. Joffre arrived in the United States in April as part of an official French mission led by former prime minister René Viviani. They addressed Congress and met with American political and military leaders, offering advice on how the United States could best assist the war effort. Unlike the British Mission, which advocated feeding American soldiers as replacements into the British Army, Joffre advocated for a separate American expeditionary force and the immediate creation of a combat division to show the flag in France (this would become the 1st Division). The monument to Major General Lafayette, beloved French hero of the American Revolution, was completed in 1924. (Both, courtesy of the Maryland Historical Society.)

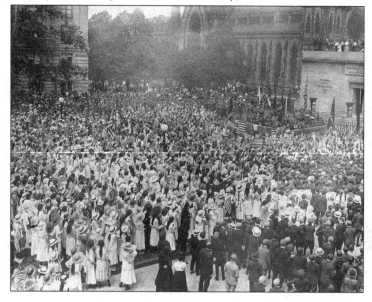

ST. HELENA
ST. HELENA, MARYLAND

PLATE LETTER K- AUGUST 15, 1918
VIEW LOOKING EAST FROM POINT K
THE DUNDALK CO. PHOTOGRAPHER

On July 1, 1918, housing construction work began for the "city of Dundalk," a new community for shipyard workers built by the Dundalk and Liberty Housing Companies. The US government, through the Emergency Fleet Corporation, funded construction with a 10-year loan to Baltimore County. Due to high rent, many residences went unoccupied. In August 1919, the homes were offered for sale to the public. (Courtesy of the Maryland Historical Society.)

In February 1918, the Ordnance Department purchased land near Perryville, at Perry Point, for construction of a massive ammonium nitrate plant operated by Atlas Powder Company. To house plant workers, the government built an entire community, complete with schools and a commissary, including these bungalows overlooking the Susquehanna. In March 1919, Perry Point became a federal hospital facility, a role that continues today under the Department of Veterans Affairs. (NARA.)

On April 6, 1918, the first anniversary of America's entry into the war, President Wilson officially opened the nation's Third Liberty Loan drive with a military parade and speech in Baltimore, capping a week of kickoff festivities there. Security surrounds the president and his entourage at the viewing stand near Union Station (now Penn Station). Below, from left to right, are former governor Edwin Warfield, Gov. Emerson C. Harrington, President Wilson, First Lady Edith Wilson, and Mayor Preston. Governor Harrington had established Maryland's Preparedness and Survey Commission as war fears escalated in February 1917, and that organization evolved into the Maryland Council of Defense after Congress declared war. The governor vigorously encouraged Maryland's war effort, calling the conflict with Germany a "holy war." (Both, LOC.)

During the parade, the 79th Division from Camp Meade, soon to depart for France, marched down East Mount Royal Avenue and past the presidential reviewing stand. The horse-drawn carts contrast sharply with the brand-new Army Standard B Liberty three-ton trucks, not to mention the numerous automotive businesses lining Mount Royal Avenue. Only the most distant buildings on the right still stand, at the corner of North Charles Street. (LOC.)

The highlight of the Third Liberty Loan drive was a joint Canadian-American series of spectacles collectively called the "Over There" Cantonment. It was centered on a set of life-size battlefield vignettes constructed at the 5th Regiment Armory, including trenches and a Red Cross bunker. For 40¢ (including a quarter toward a Liberty Bond), visitors could enter the armory and get a guided tour by a Canadian veteran. (LOC.)

SEE REAL WARFARE "OVER THERE" CANTONMENT
MADE POSSIBLE BY BLOOD-NOT MONEY
5TH REGIMENT ARMORY
BALTIMORE
OPENS MARCH 30TH
Moving Pictures
Music
Worlds greatest Orators
TICKETS FOR SALE HERE
Lloyd Harrison

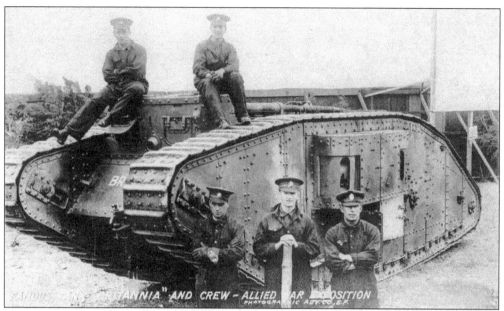

Visitors who trekked to Pimlico on April 6 could watch live demonstrations of infantry, aerial dogfighting, and *Britannia*, a British Mark IV tank. *Britannia* wowed spectators across the United States and Canada, participating in parades and demolishing cars and other obstacles. The crew were all wounded British veterans. Getting a photograph atop the tank was a real treat, and it was a major draw at recruiting and fundraising events. (Author's collection.)

Rising above the painstakingly reconstructed battlefields in the 5th Regiment Armory was this elaborate model of the Statue of Liberty, its base inscribed with the names of fallen Maryland servicemen. All of the displays were sculpted by Baltimorean Edward Henry Berge. Tickets to the Saturday-to-Saturday 5th Regiment Armory display went on advance sale on March 22 at local department stores, with over 600,000 customers prior to opening day. (NHHC.)

Baltimore's Mayor Preston (far left), George Creel of the Committee on Public Information (second from left), and Van Lear Black of Cumberland (second from right) pose with two aviators and their Standard JR-1 biplane. The aircraft is adorned with Third Liberty Loan posters and probably flew during the Baltimore festivities. Creel was effectively the US government's chief propagandist, while Black was chairman of the A.S. Abell Company (publisher of the *Baltimore Sun*) and Maryland's Liberty Loan Committee. (LOC.)

Capt. Percival Dodge of the Aviation Section, US Army Signal Corps, takes off from Pimlico Race Track in a Curtiss JN-6 "Jenny" during a staged test of Baltimore's air defenses on June 25, 1918. He then intercepted a "German bomber" (a US Army mail plane) that was performing mock attacks on city landmarks. Captain Dodge had earlier performed an aerobatic show during the Third Liberty Loan events in Baltimore. (NARA.)

Baltimore's Women's Motor Messenger Service began operating shortly after America entered the war, and by the end of 1917 had 60 volunteer drivers serving as official couriers for war activities. Organized by Capt. Vera Gamble (first row, second from left), the civilian service consisted of society women and utilized vehicles provided by the Red Cross and other organizations. (NARA.)

Pilot Max Miller of the Air Mail Service takes off from College Park Field in a Standard JR-1B mail plane on August 12, 1918. The flight inaugurated routine airmail service by the US Post Office Department, taking over the responsibility from the US Army's Air Service. Flying the mail remained extremely dangerous for years to come, and a crash would take Miller's life in 1920. (Courtesy of the Smithsonian's National Postal Museum.)

Theodore Roosevelt, the popular former president and outspoken pro-Allied belligerent, was the star of Maryland's Fourth Liberty Loan rally, exhorting the nation to "back our boys" before an audience of about 18,000 at Oriole Park (in present-day Charles Village–Abell) on September 28, 1918. The grieving colonel wore a black armband in remembrance of his youngest son, Quentin, a US Army aviator killed in France. (Courtesy of the Theodore Roosevelt Center, Dickinson State University.)

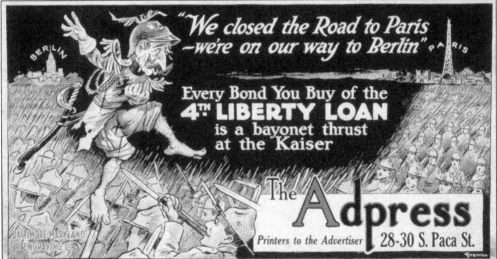

Propaganda posters featuring dehumanizing caricatures of the enemy—particularly Kaiser Wilhelm II—ranged from the grotesque to the comical. This poster was part of the massive advertising campaign for the Liberty Loans, overseen by the Committee on Public Information, which pioneered many modern psychological advertising techniques. The Liberty Loans proved enormously successful, raising over $17 billion from 20 million contributors and funding two thirds of the war effort. (LOC.)

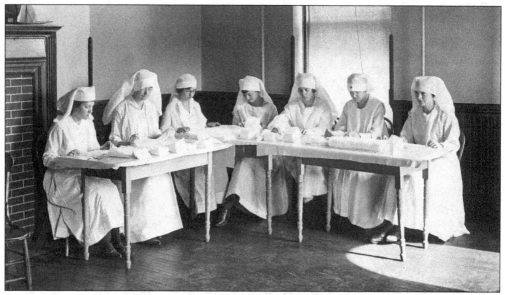

Goucher College received praise from the Committee on Public Information for its patriotism and war relief efforts, which included these students making surgical dressings for the Red Cross. Teams of volunteers competed to be the most efficient. The college also provided knitted goods, delivered periodicals to service personnel, and raised relief funds. President Wilson's middle daughter, Jessie, was a Goucher alumna, and her older sister, Margaret, had also attended. (NARA.)

Johns Hopkins Reserve Officer Training Corps (ROTC) cadets studying military engineering construct trenches on campus. In September 1918, the War Department effectively militarized many schools, including Hopkins, drafting all qualified non-ROTC students into the Student Army Training Corps (SATC). University activities were interrupted by the influenza pandemic in October, and the unexpected quick termination of the war led the War Department to abruptly dissolve the SATC after the Armistice. (NARA.)

The War Camp Community Service (WCCS) was a secular organization that sought to guide service personnel toward wholesome, morally acceptable recreational activities, part of a broader network of relief organizations that included the Red Cross, Young Men's Christian Association (YMCA), and American Library Association. The WCCS sponsored dances, sports, and other forms of entertainment. It also operated information booths such as this one and oversaw recreational facilities across Baltimore. (Author's collection.)

Segregation left the WCCS fighting an uphill battle to cater to African American soldiers, as many facilities were whites-only; patriotism often stopped short of racial tolerance. The organization operated this "Colored Club" at St. Mary's Church on Orchard Street in Baltimore, providing lodging and sponsoring social events. The old church hall is now the popular Arena Playhouse, one of the country's oldest continuously operating historically African American theaters. (Author's collection.)

The United Service Club at 204–206 West Fayette Street opened on November 10, 1917, charging soldiers and sailors 25¢ per night for comfortable, homey lodging. Amenities included baths, smoking and reading rooms, and this pool hall. Many of the volunteer staff were mothers of servicemen. Most guests were traveling through Baltimore en route to Camp Meade and other destinations. The club ceased operations in July 1919. (Author's collection.)

Prohibition was a contentious wartime debate that split Maryland's electorate. Although Maryland ratified the 18th Amendment, many Marylanders—especially in Baltimore—were decidedly "wet." The so-called Wartime Prohibition Act (to conserve grain) did not pass Congress until after the Armistice and caused much consternation when it went into effect on July 1, 1919. This is Jefferson Liquor Company's 15 North Liberty Street store in Baltimore. (Courtesy of the Maryland Historical Society.)

Three

MARYLAND'S WARTIME INDUSTRIES

Shipyards across America and Britain engaged in fierce competition for the "world riveting record." On May 16, 1918, riveter Charles Samuel Knight of Bethlehem Shipbuilding Corporation's Sparrows Point shipyard claimed the record, driving 4,873 rivets in a nine-hour period, a record that stood for several weeks. At right is his holder-on, either Henry Holcomb or John Stewart. Knight helped build ships during both world wars. (NARA.)

Josephine Usher, sponsor of the SS *Floridian*, poses with husband William and daughter Edith prior to the vessel's launch at the Maryland Steel Company (later Bethlehem Steel) shipyard at Sparrows Point in 1915. William H.E. Usher was the superintendent of Ore Steamship Lines at Sparrows Point. Built for the American-Hawaiian Steamship Company, the *Floridian* had a short civilian career before the government acquired it for wartime service. (Author's collection.)

The US Shipping Board took over the SS *Floridian* after the declaration of war, converting it into a troopship. In 1919, the US Navy acquired the vessel, commissioning it USS *Floridian* (ID-3875). It made three trips to France in 1919, hauling cargo and returning with a total of 5,444 troops. In this view, men line the decks as they pass the Statue of Liberty en route to Hoboken. (Author's collection.)

Most ships that saw active wartime service were already building or completed when the war began. The tanker SS *Ampetco* was laid down at Sparrows Point in May 1917, taken over by the US Shipping Board, and delivered in May 1918. After brief government service, the *Ampetco* was sold. In February 1942, as the SS *Cities Service Empire*, it was sunk off the Florida coast by German submarine *U-128*. (NARA.)

After declaring war, the US government seized many vessels being built under British contract, including the SS *Cape May* at Sparrows Point, causing some diplomatic headaches. The USS *Cape May* (ID-3520) was commissioned on October 25, 1918, and arrived in France shortly after the Armistice. *Cape May* made two trips bringing American soldiers home from Europe, then passed to the US Shipping Board, and finally to private ownership. (NHHC.)

Although the US government quickly launched a massive wartime shipbuilding program under the US Shipping Board's Emergency Fleet Corporation, the war ended before most ships could be completed. The freighter SS *Hoxbar*, shown on launching day at Bethlehem's Sparrows Point yard, was laid down in May 1918, launched in February 1919, completed in June 1919, served briefly as the USS *Hoxbar*, and then passed to civilian service. (NHHC.)

The keel of the SS *Hoxie*, another freighter built for the US Shipping Board under an Emergency Fleet Corporation contract, is laid at the Bethlehem yard at Sparrows Point in July 1918. The *Hoxie* was completed too late to see wartime duty, in March 1919, but its 40-year career included service with the British Ministry of War Transport (as the *Empire Albatross*) during World War II. (NHHC.)

The freighter SS *Huachuca* is shown nearing completion at Sparrows Point. Typical of many Emergency Fleet Corporation contracts, the *Huachuca* was laid down after the Armistice, and not completed until May 1919. The US Shipping Board sold the vessel to a private concern shortly thereafter, and it served as the SS *Orinoco* and then SS *San Domingo* until 1936. Many other wartime emergency vessels were scrapped before completion. (NHHC.)

Wartime "student workers," including college students and degreed professionals with no shipbuilding experience, pose at Baltimore Dry Dock and Shipbuilding Company. They were responsible for building the seagoing tug *Ludington Patton*, from drafting to launch, gaining valuable experience that would see some men promoted to work on larger vessels. The *Ludington Patton* was launched on March 8, 1919, and was in service as the *Ascension* as recently as 2011. (NARA.)

This photograph captured no welders, only the ghostly trails of their torches, as they labored on the refrigerator ship SS *South Pole* at Baltimore Dry Dock and Shipbuilding Company at Locust Point in May 1918. The night shift ran from 6:00 p.m. to 5:30 a.m. and paid a five-percent bonus in addition to three hours of overtime. *South Pole* was another British Admiralty contract seized by the US Shipping Board. (NARA.)

The SS *South Pole* is launched at Baltimore Dry Dock and Shipbuilding Company on June 17, 1918, having taken only 40 days to construct. The US Navy acquired the vessel in November 1918 and commissioned it the USS *South Pole* (ID-3665). It made two post-Armistice voyages from New York to France and was then decommissioned and returned to the US Shipping Board. (NARA.)

Baltimore Dry Dock and Shipbuilding Company completed over three dozen vessels, mostly tankers and cargo ships, for the US Shipping Board and US Navy, including the minesweeper USS *Avocet* (AM-19). Commissioned in September 1918, *Avocet* and its sister ships saw extensive, hazardous duty clearing the North Sea Mine Barrage in 1919. *Avocet* later survived the 1941 Pearl Harbor attack, and was credited with downing a Japanese torpedo bomber. (NHHC.)

USS *Bobolink* (AM-20), also built at Baltimore Dry Dock and Shipbuilding Company, was commissioned after the Armistice. *Bobolink* served alongside its sister ships with the North Sea Mining Detachment, clearing shipping lanes of the countless mines laid during the war. On May 14, 1919, *Bobolink* was severely damaged by a mine that killed commanding officer Lt. Frank Bruce. Like *Avocet*, *Bobolink* would later survive the attack on Pearl Harbor. (NHHC.)

Workers crowd Bethlehem's Sparrows Point shipyard during an event confusingly advertised as "Flag Day" on April 6, 1918, featuring music, patriotic speeches, and presentations of special service flags to workmen. The US Shipping Board, concerned by lagging production, sought to recruit and encourage shipyard workers by emphasizing the urgency and necessity of their work in the campaign against German U-boats. The new service flags were similar to those issued to military personnel except for the words "U.S. Shipping Board—War Service." Baltimore Dry Dock and Shipbuilding Company hosted its event concurrently and earned an Honor Flag for timely production. Bethlehem would ultimately employ about 5,600 workers, and Baltimore Dry Dock about 7,600. (Both, NHHC.)

The nearly forgotten Maryland Shipbuilding Company on Bear Creek at Sollers Point had wartime contracts to build six wooden cargo ships but completed only two by the time of the Armistice. The 270-foot SS *Guilford* and SS *Arundel* were Ferris-design steamers launched on October 15, 1918, and January 11, 1919, respectively. Another two ships were finished as barges, while the last two were cancelled outright. The Emergency Fleet Corporation viewed the company's workmanship positively but gave low marks for management and productivity. Overall, the entire wooden shipbuilding program proved a disappointment. In July 1919, the US Shipping Board took over the yard, which had been built using federal funds, for use as a storage area for lumber and incomplete hulls. The company dissolved at about the same time. Maryland Shipbuilding employed about 900 workers at its wartime peak. (Both, NARA.)

At the American Propeller Manufacturing Company in Baltimore, workers laminate pre-cut strips of wood using hot glue and clamps, and the outline of an aircraft propeller begins to take shape. Boards for the propellers were hand-selected to ensure proper quality and balance, and the lamination had to be perfect to ensure safe operation. The company sold more than 25,000 Paragon-brand propellers to the US and Canadian governments. (NHHC.)

Workers pause for the photographer during the propeller finishing process, done almost entirely by hand. Stacks of unfinished laminated oak propellers are visible at center, surrounded by workmen sanding, polishing, and varnishing. At its wartime height, the American Propeller Works, as the company was locally known, operated four plants in Baltimore and was the largest propeller manufacturer in the country, with about 1,200 employees. (NHHC.)

Men of the 23rd Infantry, 2nd Division, fire a French Canon d'Infanterie de 37 modèle 1916 TRP during an assault in 1918. The Poole Engineering and Manufacturing Company in Texas (south of Cockeysville) produced the gun's ammunition, first under French contract and then for the US Army, which had adopted the weapon as the 37-millimeter gun M1916. Poole also produced arms and ammunition for the US Navy and Britain. (NARA.)

In 1918, Poole began manufacturing the 37-millimeter gun's barrel for the War Department and assembled 1,200 complete American-built gun units at its Maryland Pressed Steel division in Hagerstown (pictured). Only 122 were shipped overseas before the Armistice, but they remained in postwar service. The US Army tested the weapons at Clear Spring Proving Ground west of Hagerstown, a satellite facility of Aberdeen Proving Ground built specifically for that purpose. (NARA.)

The W.J. Dickey and Sons Company mill on the Patapsco River in Oella was a major supplier of cloth to the US military during the war. The factory was consumed by fire on January 25, 1918, and quickly rebuilt. That September, company president William A. Dickey lost a son, Pvt. Allen Dickey of the 313th Infantry Regiment, in combat near Montfaucon during the Meuse-Argonne Offensive. (Courtesy of Baltimore County Public Libraries.)

Mount Vernon–Woodberry Mills on the Jones Falls in Hampden also provided large quantities of cotton duck and other fabrics to the US military for uniforms, tents, and accoutrements. The company thrived during the war, despite periodic labor unrest and a boiler explosion that killed an employee in April 1918. Employment and hours increased, and the company expanded with a new rail-accessible warehouse. (Courtesy of the Maryland Historical Society.)

Bartlett-Hayward Corporation of Baltimore manufactured munitions for Britain and Russia during the neutrality period and expanded rapidly to meet demand after the United States declared war. The War Department acquired land adjacent to Carroll Park for the company's production of 155-millimeter ammunition at the location of the present Montgomery Park Business Center. Bartlett-Hayward also operated at several other wartime sites, including its main facility at Scott and McHenry Streets. (NARA.)

Bartlett-Hayward produced nearly 3.5 million 75-millimeter shrapnel artillery shells for the US government alone, shown here being fabricated at the company's South Plant in May 1918. This plant was located at Wicomico and Gunpowder Streets, southeast of Carroll Park. Bartlett-Hayward was a key supplier of shrapnel antipersonnel ammunition, and John T. Lewis and Brothers Company, also in Baltimore, supplied the shrapnel balls used in its production. (NARA.)

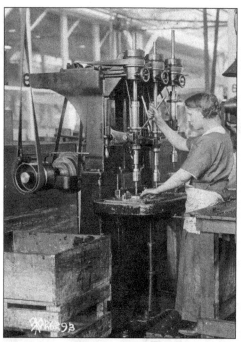

This drill press operator is helping to produce 155-millimeter shells at Bartlett-Hayward's Park Plant. Bartlett-Hayward employed over 20,000 people during the war, about one third of all munitions workers in the Baltimore area, including many women. The company produced 75-millimeter, 155-millimeter, and 4.7-inch artillery ammunition and also manufactured plant equipment for collecting the petroleum byproduct toluene, a solvent used to produce the explosive trinitrotoluene (TNT). (NARA.)

Women fill 155-millimeter shrapnel shells with explosive powder at Bartlett-Hayward's Turner Station plant. The company produced rounds for the Canon de 155 Grande Puissance Filloux (GPF) modèle 1917 long-range field artillery gun and the Canon de 155 C modèle 1917 Schneider howitzer, both French designs adopted by the US Army. However, the company delivered only 135,600 rounds, just a fraction of its 155-millimeter orders, before the war's abrupt end. (NARA.)

Workers transferring steel billets for 155-millimeter rounds at Bartlett-Hayward's Park Plant take a break to pose for the photographer. The company performed all stages of ordnance production from forging the billets to final assembly, packing, and testing, the latter stages all being accomplished at the Turner Station plant. Bartlett-Hayward's operations were serviced by the Baltimore & Ohio Railroad, which built new spur lines to link the plants. (NARA.)

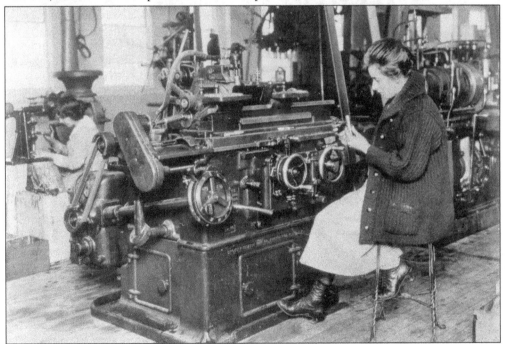

Machinists work at the Black & Decker Manufacturing Company's newly constructed Towson plant. The company, which also operated a plant on South Calvert Street, recruited "ex-schoolteachers, widows and wives of men in the service," advertising interesting work and advancement opportunities. Black & Decker pioneered handheld electric power tools and during the war manufactured breech assemblies for the 37-millimeter gun M1916. (Courtesy of Baltimore County Public Libraries and Stanley Black & Decker Inc.)

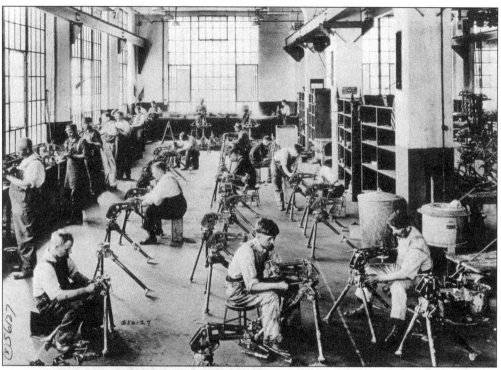

Workers assemble tripods for the Browning M1917 heavy machine gun at the Crown Cork and Seal Company's Barclay works, which turned out 100 tripods a day. The plant, at Guilford Avenue and Oliver Street, is now the Baltimore Design School. Famous for introducing the bottle cap, the Baltimore company (now Philadelphia-based Crown Holdings Inc.) also produced ammunition cartridges at its Highlandtown plant, now the Crown Industrial Park. (NARA.)

A laboratory worker tests samples at the Gibbs Preserving Company, at 2303 Boston Street in Canton. The company produced canned vegetables, ketchup, pork and beans, and oysters under the Bull Head brand. Some of the company's employees were women of the Maryland Food Reserve Corps, recruited by the Maryland Council of Defense to work the canneries for $2.40 per day. Their slogan was "Be a packer! Not a slacker!" (NARA.)

Four

MARYLAND'S MILITARY FACILITIES

Founded in 1845, the US Naval Academy in Annapolis graduated many key wartime leaders, including Adm. Henry Mayo, commander-in-chief of the Atlantic Fleet; Vice Adm. William Sims, commander-in-chief of US Naval Forces, Europe; Adm. Hugh Rodman, commander of Battleship Division 9; Adm. William Caperton, commander-in-chief of the Pacific Fleet; and Adm. Austin Knight, commander-in-chief of the Asiatic Fleet. Some wartime graduates would occupy command positions during the Second World War and Cold War. (NARA.)

The US Naval Academy class of 1918 runs through Dahlgren Hall after the hat-toss on graduation day, June 28, 1917, almost a year ahead of schedule. The class of 1917 had also graduated early, on March 29. The accelerated graduations helped ease a critical shortage of naval officers and cleared space for the training of reserve officers at the Naval Academy that summer. (NARA.)

Naval reserve officer candidates of the US Naval Academy march past their temporary barracks into Bancroft Hall on April 12, 1918. Most of these students, selected by the naval districts to further ease the critical shortage of naval officers, successfully completed accelerated coursework and received temporary reserve commissions. The Naval Academy trained five wartime reserve classes, totaling 2,569 men. (NARA.)

The Naval Academy welcomes the Japanese mission to the United States, led by special envoy Viscount Ishii Kikujiro (in bowler hat), on August 25, 1917. This was one of several official visits by the Allied powers, but tensions over recent Japanese affronts to Chinese sovereignty hung over the ceremonies. Ishii served as ambassador to the United States from 1918–1919. He was killed during an American raid on Tokyo in 1945. (LOC.)

Naval Radio Transmitting Station Annapolis, at Greenbury Point, became an unlikely popular landmark. The facility began operating in August 1918, providing secure very low frequency (VLF) radio communications to France and Britain, and served for nearly 80 years. The original four 600-foot towers, shown shortly after completion, were replaced in 1969. Eventually, 19 towers occupied the site, three of which are preserved, the rest having been demolished in 1999. (NARA.)

Naval Proving Ground Indian Head was established in 1890 and during the war was best known for testing naval guns and armor and as the home of the US Navy's smokeless powder factory (below). Less publicized, but critical, was its role in experimenting with explosives and ordnance designs. Over 4,500 guns were tested during the war, and powder production doubled, from roughly 1,500 to roughly 3,000 tons per year, between 1914 and 1918. Wartime demands led to expansion and upgrades, including a rail line, dock, and over 100 homes for personnel, who eventually numbered almost 10,000, although much of the work was incomplete at the time of the Armistice. The adjacent town of Indian Head, swelled by wartime workers, incorporated in 1920. Today the former proving ground is known as Naval Support Facility Indian Head. (Both, NARA.)

A dozen naval rifles of various sizes await proof-testing at Indian Head, with additional guns yet to be unloaded. The structure at right is a bombproof shelter in case a gun burst. Indian Head also had batteries to test velocity and range. By 1917, Indian Head was too cramped and geographically restricted to test the largest naval guns, a function soon moved to a new facility at Dahlgren, Virginia. (NARA.)

In early 1918, Naval Proving Ground Indian Head began training sailors to man the US Navy's five new massive 14-inch railway guns, which wreaked havoc on German strategic targets far behind the lines in the war's final weeks. Each mounted a standard US 14-inch, 50-caliber Mark IV battleship gun on a carriage built by Baldwin Locomotive Works and could fire a 1,400-pound projectile a distance of nearly 24 miles. (NARA.)

In April 1917, the US Navy sought a new standard machine gun. Here, Maj. Gen. George Barnett, commandant of the Marine Corps (center), operates a Colt-Browning M1895 during tests at Marine Corps Rifle Range Winthrop on Stump Neck. The American-designed Lewis gun (operated by the Marine in the foreground), already in widespread British service, won the competition. In the background are two M1909 Benét–Mercié guns. (LOC.)

Franklin Delano Roosevelt, the enthusiastic and energetic assistant secretary of the Navy and an avid marksman, also attended the weapons tests at Winthrop, as did Secretary of the Navy Josephus Daniels (aiming his rifle) and other government officials. The Winthrop range and tent encampment was a satellite facility of Indian Head Proving Ground designed for temporary use. The site is now Naval Support Facility Indian Head, Stump Neck Annex. (LOC.)

Fort Foote in Prince George's County was used to train Army Corps of Engineers personnel during the war. Men from the Washington Barracks used the site to learn trench construction and infantry skills, turning the grounds of the Civil War–era coastal defense fort into a maze of trenches. These are soldiers of the 1st Replacement Regiment Engineers training in June 1918. Trenches were zigzagged to minimize casualties in the event of an enemy penetration, preventing any one attacker from having a clear line of fire through the entire trench, and likewise to limit the effects of artillery blasts. American soldiers in France typically occupied preexisting British and French trenches. Fort Foote is now a public park administered by the National Park Service. (Both, NARA.)

Iconic Fort McHenry, which the federal government had given to the City of Baltimore in 1914, again assumed a military role in August 1917 when it became home to US Army General Hospital No. 2. The hospital grew to occupy 111 buildings, 75 being of wartime construction and the rest consisting of adjacent US Bureau of Immigration buildings and former coast defense structures. Fort McHenry specialized in surgery, particularly neurosurgery, and patient rehabilitation. It also trained US Army base hospital personnel for service overseas. The first patients from France began arriving in February 1918, and the hospital eventually expanded to hold 2,700 beds. By 1919, the hospital's busiest year, it had a staff of 78 officers, 863 enlisted men, and 123 nurses. (Above, courtesy of Fort McHenry National Monument and Historic Shrine; below, NARA.)

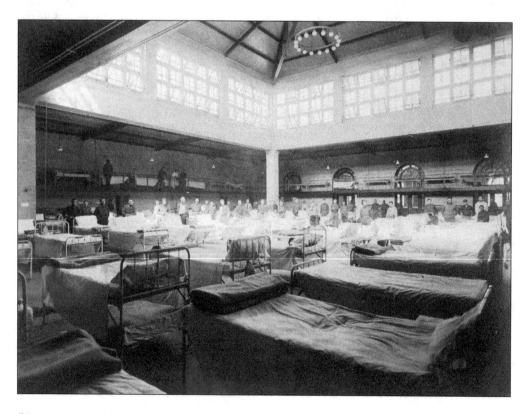

Wounded patients at Fort McHenry, many of them awaiting prostheses, pose for the photographer in 1918. At the time this photograph was taken, the mass casualties from the Meuse-Argonne Offensive had yet to begin arriving in the United States. By the end of the year, almost half of the hospital's patients required a prosthesis. In January 1919, the hospital established maxillofacial services for patients with severe facial wounds. (Both, NARA.)

Patients recovering from shell shock, now known as post-traumatic stress disorder (PTSD), weave willow baskets at Fort McHenry. Shell shock affected many veterans but was poorly understood for much of the war. The hospital's state-of-the-art neuropsychiatric service offered occupational therapy in addition to psychotherapy and hydrotherapy. The basket-weaving program was supported by Maryland's Hospital for the Negro Insane in Crownsville, which provided instruction and materials. (NARA.)

In November 1917, the US Army acquired the use of the Garrett family's estates in Roland Park (including Evergreen and Evergreen Junior) as the grounds for General Hospital No. 7. The 300-bed hospital pioneered vocational instruction for the blind, many of whom had undergone surgery and other treatment at General Hospital No. 2 at Fort McHenry. Classes included basket weaving, poultry farming, motor vehicle and tire repair, cigar making, musical performance, and carpentry. Much of the former hospital grounds are now home to Loyola University Maryland, and the Evergreen Junior manor headquarters shown above is now the university's Francis Xavier Knott Humanities Center. The Evergreen manor is now home to Johns Hopkins University's Evergreen Museum and Library. (Both, NARA.)

In addition to vocational training, General Hospital No. 7 was devoted to mentally and physically rehabilitating blinded personnel, many of them victims of artillery blasts or gas exposure. The hospital provided space for calisthenics, a swimming pool, lush gardens, and even a bowling alley. Much of the routine was designed to restore confidence, with swimming and even bowling reportedly proving effective. (NARA.)

Assisted by a Red Cross nurse, a soldier learns to read Braille while a sailor learns to type it. The American Red Cross played a major role at the hospital, and when the government demilitarized it in April 1919, the Red Cross received operational control. It was known afterward as the Red Cross Institute for the Blind at Evergreen Hospital. (LOC.)

Instructors demonstrate operation of a British Ordnance BL 9.2-inch howitzer at Aberdeen Proving Ground. The government's effort to establish the proving ground, necessitating a large area close to industry yet remote enough to remain innocuous, encountered heated opposition from farmers and landowners. The government abandoned plans for an Eastern Shore site and eventually resettled a community of some 3,000 people to make way for the sprawling facility near Aberdeen. (NARA.)

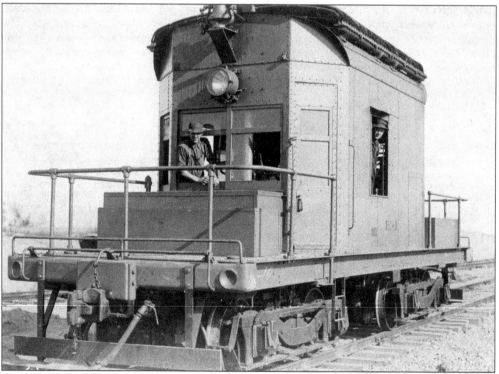

This 200-horsepower General Electric boxcab switcher, in service at Aberdeen Proving Ground, was the motive power for the Army's 16-inch howitzer M1918, one of the largest railway guns in US service at the time. Aberdeen Proving Ground, built beginning in January 1918, soon became a major Ordnance Department proof-testing center, a role that continued for many decades. (NARA.)

Aberdeen Proving Ground tested a number of railway artillery designs, including this massive 16-inch howitzer M1918. The howitzer could lob a 1,660-pound projectile to a range of over 12 miles. The test results were impressive, leading the War Department to order 61 units, but none were built before the Armistice, and the design was abandoned. (NARA.)

Personnel test a 6-inch gun M1905 at Aberdeen Proving Ground in October 1918. The War Department evaluated this seacoast defense weapon as a long-range field artillery piece, mated with several types of wheeled carriage, but found it overly heavy. Instead, the US Army adopted the French Canon de 155 GPF modèle 1917, which the US subsequently produced as the 155-millimeter gun M1918 and used through World War II. (NARA.)

Gas warfare became a prominent feature of World War I combat, and in 1918, the War Department established the US Filling Plant on Gunpowder Neck Reservation, soon known as Edgewood Arsenal (now Edgewood Chemical Biological Center). Operated by the new US Army Chemical Warfare Service, Edgewood Arsenal produced a variety of gas munitions during the war, including mustard, chlorine, phosgene, and chloropicrin gases. The latter three were considered lethal; nonlethal gases were used to disable enemy soldiers or force them to constantly wear cumbersome gas masks, causing exhaustion. Some Edgewood-produced gases were used to fill grenades and artillery shells on-site, while the rest were sent to England and France to fill munitions there. The arsenal could manufacture 550 tons of chemicals and fill 128,000 chemical munitions per day, although those capacities were never reached before the Armistice. (Both, NARA.)

Soldiers place empty 75-millimeter shells into a mustard gas filling machine. The truck in the foreground has empty shells on the left and filled shells on the right. A torch was used to incinerate any gas left on the exterior of the filled containers. Edgewood suffered four fatalities and 925 non-fatal casualties between June and December 1918, over 72 percent of injuries being from mustard gas exposure. (NARA.)

Soldiers spray paint completed gas shells. Chemical shells were painted gray and otherwise specially marked, distinguishing them from other ordnance. These are 75-millimeter "NC" shells, filled with a mixture of 80 percent chloropicrin and 20 percent stannic chloride, identified by white, red, and yellow bands. In the background at left are several larger rounds for the Livens Projector, the standard British gas mortar, also adopted by the US Army. (NARA.)

Camp Holabird was late to war service, with construction beginning in June 1918. Named after former quartermaster general Brig. Gen. Samuel Holabird, a Civil War veteran, Holabird was a Motor Transport Corps camp responsible for training and vehicle shipments. This scene conveys some sense of the scale of the camp's operations, with over 250 Mack Brothers Model AC trucks awaiting disposition. The Mack AC "Bulldog" saw extensive wartime service. (LOC.)

US Army firefighters of Camp Holabird's Engine Company No. 1 pose with their new Dodge-Pirsch chemical cars in 1918. By 1919, Camp Holabird had become a major motor transport center, including storage yards and a massive repair depot. After the war, it even began manufacturing its own line of fire apparatus based on surplus Liberty trucks. (NARA.)

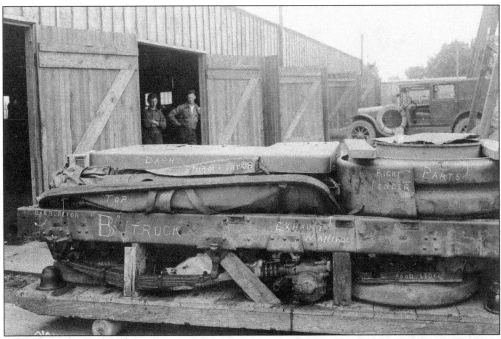

Some of the vehicles shipped by Camp Holabird were disassembled and crated for reassembly overseas. Above is a US Army Standard B Liberty truck loaded onto a pallet, each component identified with chalk, which was later enclosed with plywood. Below, fully crated trucks are stacked awaiting shipment to occupation forces after the Armistice. The Liberty truck was a standardized three-ton, two-wheel-drive design, the brainchild of a cooperative effort between the Ordnance Corps, the Society of Automotive Engineers, and manufacturers, and was produced by 15 different firms during the war. (Both, NARA.)

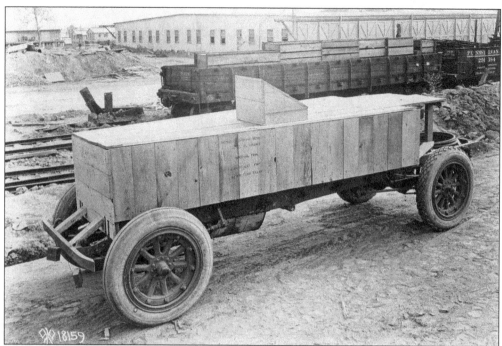

Crated in a less time-consuming fashion is this White Motor Company Model 15 three-quarter-ton truck awaiting shipment. The American effort to produce and ship motor vehicles never reached its full potential before the Armistice. During the war, less than half of the AEF's vehicles were American-built, and units still relied in part on horse-drawn transport. (NARA.)

Soldiers of the 601st Engineer Regiment construct a pontoon bridge across Marley Creek during a drill at Camp Glenburnie. The tent encampment at Glenburnie (now Glen Burnie) was collocated with the Maryland State Rifle Range (Saunders Range), which was leased to the Navy Department and served as Naval Rifle Range Glenburnie during the war. The 601st organized at Camp Laurel and arrived in France in June 1918. (NARA.)

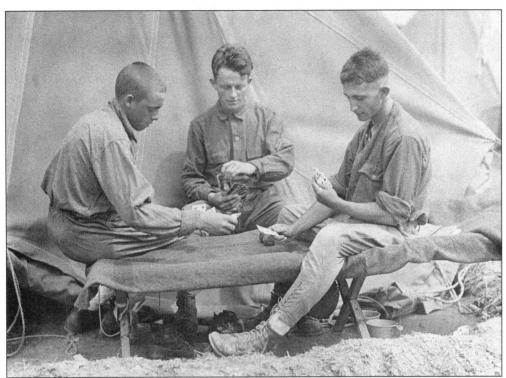

Soldiers of the 4th Maryland Infantry play pitch at Camp Laurel, their temporary mobilization encampment at Laurel Park. The regiment departed for Camp McClellan, Alabama, by train on September 16, 1917. By that time, preparations were already underway for the upcoming Maryland State Fair horse races. The historic 4th Maryland would not fight together as a unit, instead being parceled out to various components of the 29th Division. (Author's collection.)

Camp Laurel soon emerged as a subsidiary US Army engineer camp, taking overflow from nearby Camp Meade. The 23rd, 57th, 66th, and 601st Engineer Regiments were recruited and organized at Camp Laurel, occupying both a tent encampment and the Maryland State Fair buildings. The 57th, whose recruiting poster is shown, operated a river transportation network in France beginning in the summer of 1918. Camp Laurel closed in January 1919. (LOC.)

General Supply Ordnance Depot, Reserve, Curtis Bay (later known as Curtis Bay Ordnance Depot) was built during 1918 to house munitions. The federal government had acquired the land prior to the declaration of war, in 1916. In addition to its depot functions, the facility played a minor role in troop mobilization, briefly hosting the 50th Infantry Regiment, which participated in the occupation of Germany from 1919 to 1921. (NARA.)

Railroad personnel pose with an Ordnance Department 0-4-0 switcher at Curtis Bay. The Baltimore & Ohio Railroad serviced the depot, with spur lines running to each warehouse. The depot was utilized for many decades, and a number of the original warehouse buildings still stand, although most are badly deteriorated. A large portion of the site remains federally owned, including the 1SG Brandt US Army Reserve Center. (NARA.)

Five

CAMP MEADE

New draftees arrive by rail at Camp Meade in 1917. Under the Selective Service Act of 1917, over 2.8 million men were drafted, amounting to nearly three fifths of all military personnel by war's end. From a paltry 208,000 men in April 1917, the US Army (including the National Guard) would swell to nearly 3.7 million in less than two years. (LOC.)

Camp Meade, named for Maj. Gen. George Gordon Meade, the Civil War hero who led the Army of the Potomac during the Battle of Gettysburg, was one of the newly established training centers for new National Army units. It was originally built to organize and train the 79th Division, which, like the other National Army divisions, was composed predominantly of draftees, augmenting the Regular Army and National Guard. Begun on July 18, 1917, its training grounds and more than 2,000 structures occupied 9,349 acres carved out of what was then mostly rural farmland along the rail line between Admiral and Annapolis Junction. The press called it Maryland's "second city." In 1919, Camp Meade became a major demobilization center for returning units and briefly hosted the US Army's tank school. Today it is Fort George G. Meade, a major defense installation hosting various intelligence and information technology activities, including the National Security Agency. (NARA.)

Draftees make their way into the camp to receive uniforms and equipment. Camp Meade primarily took draftees from the eastern half of the United States, with 44,153 coming from Pennsylvania and 24,604 from Maryland. Although National Army units like the 79th Division were initially regional, that began to change as the Army expanded. By the time they arrived overseas, most "Maryland" units contained men from many states. (NARA.)

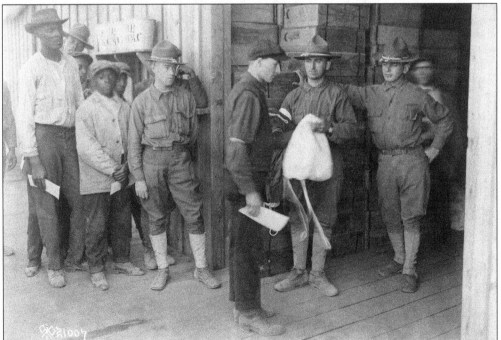

After receiving their uniform tickets, draftees' first stop was to receive barracks bags. They were then fitted and issued shoes and uniforms, marking the transition from civilian to doughboy (a slang term whose origins are unclear but which became the enduring moniker for the American World War I soldier). The first draftees arrived at Meade in September 1917, just weeks after construction of the camp began. (NARA.)

While basic obstacle courses promoted physical fitness, agility, and teamwork (above), Camp Meade also had an elaborate obstacle course featuring trenches and hanging fascines for bayonet practice (below). Bayonet drills were primarily intended to foster an aggressive, martial spirit, since the bayonet itself had become a relatively minor weapon. Still, the drills represented American "open warfare" tactics that critics viewed as outdated and foolhardy. Infantrymen were optimistically expected to dash across open ground, making use of aimed rifle fire (and bayonets when necessary), in order to finally break the deadlock of defensive trench warfare. Without proper artillery support, however, such tactics would prove costly in the face of well-placed enemy machine guns. (Both, NARA.)

British captain James P. O'Donovan leads men of the 2nd Battalion, 368th Infantry, in a bayonet drill. The 368th Infantry, 92nd Division, was activated at the camp in November 1917. This unit would later be infamously besmirched after failing to meet expectations during the Meuse-Argonne Offensive, which several racist commanders attributed to racial inferiority despite similar experiences among a number of white units during the often chaotic battle. (NARA.)

A seven-man infantry support gun crew drills with its 37-millimeter gun M1916, complete with wheeled carriage and armored shield. Three gun crews were assigned to each regimental headquarters company. Photographs indicate that in forward areas, American soldiers typically used the gun on its fixed tripod and without the armor shield. It could fire 25 rounds per minute and had an effective range of about 1,500 yards. (NARA.)

Machine gunners practice with wooden mock-ups and (in the foreground) one actual Colt-Vickers M1915, the license-built American version of the famous British Vickers machine gun. Each division had three machine gun battalions (including one for each infantry brigade), and each infantry regiment had an additional machine gun company, a total of about 260 guns per division. American machine gun units fielded an assortment of American, French, and British weapons. (NARA.)

Riflemen go "over the top" with bayonets fixed during a live-fire exercise. They carry the M1917, the American version of the British Pattern 1914 Enfield rifle (which was also mainly produced in the United States). The M1917 became the standard rifle of the AEF, temporarily outnumbering the more famous M1903 Springfield in frontline units. (NARA.)

Sous lieutenant Paul Rochat (left) and Adjudant Garman demonstrate the innovative but temperamental Chauchat light machine gun for American trainees. Rochat was an automatic weapons specialist and veteran of the French 113e regiment d'infanterie, wounded twice in battle. AEF soldiers despised the poorly engineered "Sho-Sho," which frequently jammed. The 79th Division was one of the first to be equipped with its replacement, the superb Browning Automatic Rifle. (NARA.)

Field artillery crews trained with either obsolete equipment or wooden mock-ups of their weapons, in this case the famous French 75-millimeter (Canon de 75 modèle 1897). Most artillerists only received and began training with their actual weapons after they reached France. The US Army adopted the excellent "French 75," and American firms began producing it under license, but few American-built guns had reached France by war's end. (NARA.)

World War I saw the birth of mechanized warfare, and doughboys were often transported on trucks like this artillery convoy's Four Wheel Drive Auto Company Model B. Soldiers would find that muddy French roads, especially after years of shelling by German artillery, were insufficient to move the required quantities of men and materiel to the front. During the Meuse-Argonne Offensive, many roads became hopelessly clogged, creating a logistical nightmare. (LOC.)

Horses are loaded into railcars at Auxiliary Remount Depot No. 304. Each major camp had such a depot, operated by the US Army Remount Service, Quartermaster Corps, responsible for collecting, caring for, and shipping horses and mules to units at other camps or overseas as needed. Depot No. 304 was equipped to house 12,000 animals. The military still relied heavily on horses, despite advances in mechanized warfare. (LOC.)

Men of the 304th Field Signal Battalion practice establishing a field telephone station, complete with horse-drawn cable cart, semaphore signalman, and motorcycle dispatch riders. The motorcycles are Harley-Davidsons, and the field telephone/telegraph is the Service Buzzer Model 1914. The 304th was the 79th Division's signal battalion and saw service during the Meuse-Argonne Offensive. Maintaining lines of communication was critical, and wire communications technology often failed commanders during combat operations. Lines were frequently cut by shelling or enemy infiltrators or shorted out by water. In August 1918, construction began on the subsidiary Camp Benjamin Franklin, a dedicated Signal Corps facility adjacent to Camp Meade, but it was not occupied until the last two weeks of the war. (Both, NARA.)

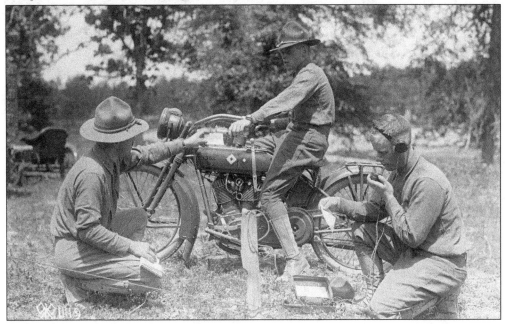

The rustic 79th Division Headquarters building hosted this gigantic Second Liberty Loan "clock" charting the camp's contributions. Every soldier was encouraged to participate in the loan-buying program, and on November 5, 1917, the *Baltimore Sun* reported that Camp Meade led all other National Army posts in per capita contributions. The Camp Meade average was $89.39, for a total of $1,607,800. (LOC.)

Camp Meade's "Hello Girls," as female switchboard operators were known, staffed the post's telephone exchange from its earliest days until 1921. Forty-eight women of the Chesapeake & Potomac (C&P) Telephone Company worked in three shifts during the war, many commuting via the Washington, Baltimore & Annapolis Electric Railway, and dormitories were provided to overnight shift workers. Contact with soldiers at Camp Meade was strictly forbidden until after the Armistice. (NARA.)

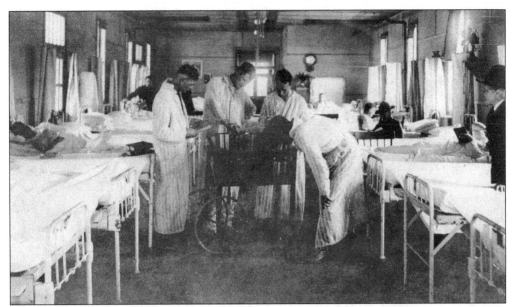

The Camp Meade Base Hospital was formed in August 1917 and began receiving patients in September. In its first three months, most admissions were for infectious disease, over half of which were venereal disease patients. The 1,930-bed hospital had a staff of 89 medical officers, 721 enlisted men, and 221 nurses. Here, convalescents check books out from an American Library Association cart. (NARA.)

Although Camp Meade's surgical ward (pictured) kept busy with wounded and injured patients, the post's most serious medical challenge came from influenza. Maryland's first cases were reported there on September 17, 1918. Camp Meade ultimately suffered nearly 10,000 cases and at least 60 fatalities. Several thousand died statewide, the influx of patients overwhelming every medical facility. The pandemic killed upwards of 30 million worldwide, including an estimated 675,000 Americans. (NARA.)

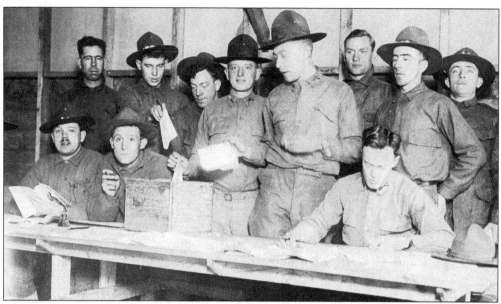

Soldiers exercise their right to vote, likely Pennsylvanians participating in the election of November 6, 1917. Whereas Pennsylvania made arrangements for its men in military camps to vote, Maryland ultimately offered no such option, disenfranchising many voters. Maj. Gen. Joseph E. Kuhn, commanding both Camp Meade and the 79th Division, foresaw chaos and felt it unwise to allow soldiers to leave camp en masse to cast ballots. (NARA.)

The American Library Association was actively involved at US Army cantonments and operated this roughly 15,000-volume War Service Library and 18 branches at Camp Meade, the latter located at various recreational facilities. The library emphasized scientific and technical books of potential value to modern soldiers but relied on donations, which to its chagrin occasionally included extraneous attic discards and even pro-German and anti-war propaganda (which were promptly burned). (LOC.)

Jewish soldiers attend a chaplain's lecture after Rosh Hashanah services in September 1918. The Jewish Welfare Board, US Army and Navy (JWB), worked in cooperation with the War and Navy Departments and oversaw chapels and services at military installations. The JWB also played a key role in recruiting chaplains and lay workers, many of whom served overseas. (NARA.)

Cardinal James Gibbons, the popular and influential archbishop of Baltimore, conducts mass during one of his camp visits. Maryland has deep Catholic roots, but the nationwide level of hostility toward non-Protestants at that time is often forgotten today. Anti-Catholic and anti-Semitic sentiments in particular were rampant during the war, and for many years afterward, making organizations like the Knights of Columbus and Jewish Welfare Board all the more important. (NARA.)

Spurred by Herbert Hoover, head of the US Food Administration, who actively sought to avoid wartime shortages, the 79th Division at Camp Meade instituted a strict conservation and recycling program. Soldiers could be penalized for wastefulness. These rows of cans to collect reusable discards were placed outside every mess facility. (LOC.)

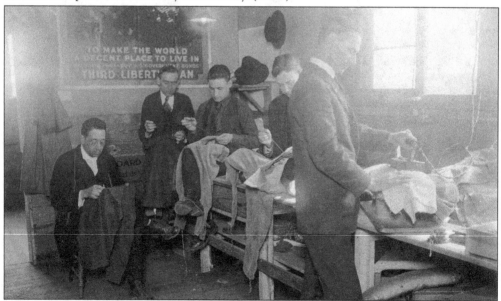

Clothing was also conserved whenever possible. In addition to larger Quartermaster Corps base salvage plants, such as those in Baltimore and Washington, DC, each camp had clothing and hat repair shops. These men are mending damaged uniforms at Camp Meade's Salvage Division. The Quartermaster Corps estimated that it saved nearly $57 million from its total salvage operations during the period from July 1, 1918, to June 30, 1919. (NARA.)

As the Army expanded, so did its demand for coffee, presenting technological and logistical challenges. Here, soldiers feed coffee beans into Camp Meade's massive roaster, capable of delivering 6,000 pounds of coffee every 10 hours. The roaster, manufactured by Jabez Burns and Sons of New York, was the largest type in US Army service. (NARA.)

A camp mess facility receives a welcome shipment from Baltimore's Schmidt Bakery, now Schmidt Baking Company, which was then a division of the combined City Baking Company. In addition to its extensive mess halls for units in training, Camp Meade also housed a bakers and cooks school that trained seven Quartermaster Corps bakery companies during the war. (NARA.)

Men of the 11th "Lafayette" Division pose for a living insignia shot by a photographer atop a tall scaffold, an art form in vogue during World War I and still occasionally seen today. The letters were formed with campaign hats. The 11th Division, a mix of Regular Army and National Army units, organized at Camp Meade in August 1918 and was about 24,000 strong when the Armistice took effect. Marylanders served throughout the division, and its 72nd Infantry and 33rd Field Artillery Regiments were largely comprised of Maryland draftees. Only an advance detachment went overseas before the war ended, arriving in England on November 8, and the division was demobilized by February 7, 1919. (Author's collection.)

Six

MARYLAND MILITARY UNITS

Men of Maryland's 117th Trench Mortar Battery, part of the 42nd "Rainbow" Division, load their weapon during a joint French-American raid in March 1918. They are equipped with the French 58-millimeter Type 2 medium mortar. The assault on German trenches near Badonviller was a brief flash of violence in an otherwise relatively quiet sector. The 117th, composed of National Guard coast artillerists, was the first Maryland unit to enter combat. (NARA.)

The 115th Infantry Regiment, part of the 58th Infantry Brigade, 29th Division, practices marching in review at Camp McClellan, Alabama, in February 1918. The 115th Infantry was organized in October 1917 from Maryland's National Guard infantry regiments, which had arrived at Camp McClellan in September. The new 29th Division, National Guard, drawn from both northern and southern states, was designated the "Blue and Gray" Division. (NARA.)

British sergeant major William Madden demonstrates bayonet techniques to men of the 115th Infantry at Camp McClellan near Anniston, Alabama. The regiment was popularly known as "Maryland's Own." Most of its men came from the 1st and 5th Maryland Infantry Regiments, which claimed lineage to militia units organized in 1775 and 1774 respectively. Its successor is the 175th Infantry Regiment, still known as the "Fifth Maryland." (Author's collection.)

The colors of the 313th Infantry Regiment, 79th Division, are presented on behalf of the citizens of Allegany County during a ceremony at Camp Meade on April 4, 1918, received by Color Sgt. Charles A. Leidlich of Baltimore. Many Allegany County men served in the 313th, a National Army regiment predominantly filled by Maryland draftees, but they were outnumbered by Baltimoreans, who gave the regiment the title "Baltimore's Own." (NARA.)

Soldiers of "Baltimore's Own" practice bayonet assault at Camp Meade. Men of the 79th Division were frequently transferred to fill other units, their places taken by new draftees from Maryland and elsewhere. Moreover, many of its officers had been hastily promoted from within the Regular Army. When they left for France, some 58 percent of the 79th Division were new recruits with only a few weeks of training. (NARA.)

The USS *Missouri* (BB-11), an obsolete *Maine*-class battleship mounting four 12-inch guns in two turrets, served as a training ship during the war. Manned partially by the Maryland Naval Militia and based in the Chesapeake Bay, the *Missouri* trained gunnery and engineering personnel destined for service on active ships, including armed merchant vessels. At war's end, the *Missouri* transported 3,278 soldiers home from France during four trips in 1919. (NARA.)

The US Navy commissioned the USS *Dorchester* (SP-1509), an 1893 bugeye leased from the Conservation Commission of Maryland, on August 24, 1917. That month, the Conservation Commission's entire State Fishery Force and its vessels were inducted as Squadron 8 of the US 5th Naval District. Maryland's "Oyster Navy" (a name dating back to the Oyster Wars of the 1800s) patrolled the state's waterways throughout the war. (NHHC.)

Mortarmen of the 117th Trench Mortar Battery maneuver their weapon into position during training in France. The 117th was comprised of men from the 3rd and 4th Companies, Maryland Coast Artillery Corps. It was part of the 42nd Division, called the "Rainbow" Division because its components were drawn from multiple states' National Guard units. (NARA.)

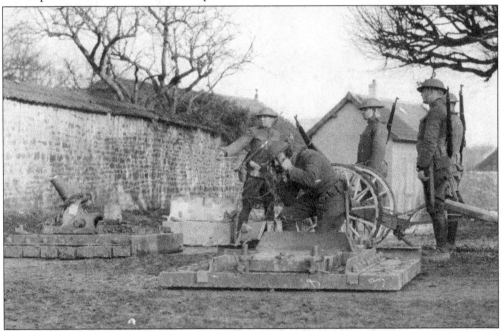

The 117th Trench Mortar Battery practices firing procedure at Neuilly, France, in February 1918. Each mortar section had two detachments of five men: a gunner (holding the lanyard) and four cannoneers. The battery commander (with telephone) directed the operation of the mortars, providing the required barrel elevation and type of projectile, propelling charge, and fuse. With typical ordnance, the mortar had a range of 100 to 1,250 meters. (NARA.)

Noncommissioned officers of Headquarters, 372nd Infantry, pose after arriving in France in April 1918. The 372nd Infantry was formed around a nucleus of National Guard units, including Maryland's 1st Separate Company, Infantry, which became Company I and also contributed headquarters personnel. The 1st Separate Company was the successor to Baltimore's Monumental City Guard. Unwelcomed by prejudiced American generals, the 372nd would instead earn battle honors under French command. (Author's collection.)

American soldiers recovering from gas attacks are treated to chocolates at Red Cross Hospital No. 5 in Auteuil. The 93rd Division (Provisional), which included the 372nd Infantry, was uniquely equipped with French accoutrements, including the iconic blue Adrian helmet. The 93rd never served as a unit, the 372nd Infantry instead seeing fierce combat as part of the French 157e division d'infanterie, the famous "Main Rouge" (Red Hand) Division. (NARA.)

Many Maryland employees of C&P Telephone enlisted together in Company D, 403rd Telegraph Battalion, which arrived in France in June 1918. The companies of the Bell Telephone System cooperated with the US Army to establish a Signal Reserve Corps of skilled telephone and telegraph specialists. (NARA.)

Men of Company D, 403rd Telegraph Battalion, train at Camp Sherman, Ohio, before deploying to France. The 403rd established and maintained lines south of Paris and later near Verdun as the Allies advanced. After the Armistice, they linked Allied and German lines, even repairing damaged German equipment to facilitate connections. (NARA.)

US Army Base Hospital 18, comprised of personnel from Johns Hopkins Hospital, was the first Maryland unit to arrive in France, disembarking on June 28, 1917. Its 27 officers, 153 enlisted men, and 65 nurses (58 of whom posed for this photograph) occupied a former French hospital at Bazoilles-sur-Meuse, which eventually expanded to 1,300 beds. The Baltimore Red Cross played a major role in equipping the new unit. (NARA.)

All but two of Base Hospital 18's officers, Johns Hopkins doctors and instructors who had accepted commissions in the US Army, posed for this photograph before leaving for France. Many of the enlisted men who served under them were Johns Hopkins medical students. For several months, Base Hospital 18 had sole responsibility for the sick and wounded of the US First Army, which was then in training. (NARA.)

US Army Base Hospital 42 was comprised of personnel from the University of Maryland Medical School. It mobilized at Camp Meade in April 1918 with 34 officers (all but two of whom posed for this photograph), 200 enlisted men, and 102 nurses, and arrived at Bazoilles-sur-Meuse in July 1918. The first patients began arriving within days. Base Hospital 42 normally had 1,000 beds and specialized in maxillofacial surgery. (NARA.)

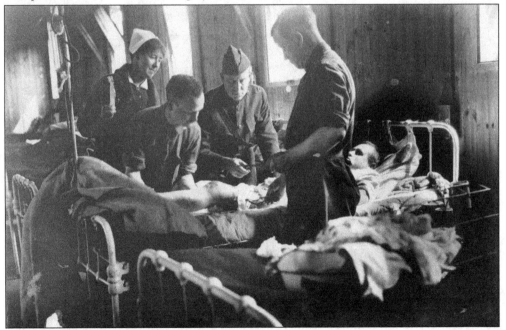

Doctors of Base Hospital 18 perform surgery on a wounded soldier in May 1918, a period of increasing American activity on the front. In July, the hospital's role shifted, as Bazoilles-sur-Meuse grew to become a massive hospital complex housing multiple base hospitals. Base Hospital 18 would thereafter specialize in chest and abdominal surgery, as well as treatment of contagious disease, treating a total of 14,179 patients during the war. (NARA.)

Convalescents enjoy some fresh air at Base Hospital 18 on May 2, 1918. At that point, the United States had yet to mount a major attack, but casualties from shelling and enemy raids increased as Americans began entering frontline trenches. The hospital itself received relatively few patients until the Meuse-Argonne Offensive, although its personnel staffed busy frontline surgical evacuation hospitals during the Battles of Château-Thierry and Saint-Mihiel. (NARA.)

This photograph shows some of the dramatic July 1918 expansion of the Bazoilles-sur-Meuse hospital complex. The facility received so many severely wounded patients during the Meuse-Argonne Offensive that its units often functioned as evacuation hospitals, sending as many cases as possible to hospitals in rear areas. Despite operating beyond capacity, Base Hospitals 18 and 42 still provided detachments to other hospitals, including evacuation hospitals at the front when needed. (NARA.)

Maj. Gen. Charles G. Morton, commanding general of the 29th Division (center), and Brig. Gen. Harry H. Bandholtz, then commanding the 58th Infantry Brigade (center right, in helmet), inspect the 115th Infantry near Montreux-Vieux, Alsace (then part of Germany), on August 29, 1918. The regiment was attached to the French Army, occupying defenses north of the Swiss border until repositioning to the northwest just prior to the Meuse-Argonne Offensive. (NARA.)

Marylanders comprised about one fifth of the 79th Division's 304th Mobile Ordnance Repair Shop, where Lt. Val Browning of Utah prepares to test-fire a newly repaired Browning Automatic Rifle, designed by his father. On September 22, 1918, Cpl. Joseph Oppitz (Baltimore), Pfc. John Rhodes (Govans), and Pvt. Joseph Wright (Hebron), Company E, 313th Infantry, introduced the now-famous weapon to combat, earning division citations for gallantry for repulsing a German raid. (NARA.)

The Meuse-Argonne Offensive, launched on September 26, 1918, was the costliest and arguably largest battle in American history, involving about 1.2 million men, over 122,000 of whom were casualties, including 26,277 killed. Pershing hoped that a lightning assault would break through a key German defensive position, the Kreimhilde Stellung (named after a character from Norse mythology). The heights of Montfaucon d'Argonne, dominated by the infamous mansion at left, which concealed a German artillery observation post, and the fortified church ruins at right, were one of the 79th Division's D-Day objectives and the most formidable obstacle to the initial American advance. From the heights, the Germans had an unparalleled view of the entire Verdun sector, site of one of the war's largest, longest, and deadliest battles in 1916, in which some 300,000 men had perished. The French believed that it would take three months to seize the heavily fortified "Little Gibraltar." Pershing optimistically ordered it taken within seven hours. "Baltimore's Own" 313th Infantry, in its first battle, reached the summit after nearly a day and a half of savage fighting. (NARA.)

Soldiers examine a German 15-centimeter sFH 02 howitzer position at smoke-shrouded Montfaucon soon after the heights were taken. The important German observation post, which helped direct artillery across the Verdun front, was formidably defended by artillery, machine gun nests, and concealed pillboxes, linked by a network of tunnels and trenches. Beyond Montfaucon, the depleted 79th Division hurled itself against the Kreimhilde Stellung for three bloody days without success. (Author's collection.)

Company G, 313th Infantry, patrols near Combres-sous-les-Côtes in the Troyon Defensive Sector on October 23, 1918. After being decimated in vain attempts to surmount the Kreimhilde Stellung, the 313th was relieved and spent October performing relatively quiet duty, although German shelling continued to inflict casualties, killing 27 and wounding 110. The battered regiment returned to the front on October 31 and resumed the attack on November 7. (NARA.)

Support elements of the 115th Infantry advance into the newly occupied ruins of Brabant-sur-Meuse on October 10, 1918. The 115th, temporarily attached to the French 18e division, was fighting to secure the heights on the east side of the Meuse River, meeting fierce resistance in the Bois de Consenvoye (Consenvoye Woods) and at Molleville Farm. The regiment lost 183 killed and 665 wounded during the Meuse-Argonne Offensive from October 2 to 31. (NARA.)

Some Germans, having endured years at the front, deserted to Allied lines in hopes of a happier future, as this *soldat* did near Mouilly, France, in October 1918. He is escorted by Sgt. Julius Keim of Baltimore, Company M, 313th Infantry (left), and Pvt. Arthur McCain of the Intelligence Section, 79th Division Headquarters. Sergeant Keim and the German are both wearing gas mask cases around their necks. (NARA.)

The 314th Ambulance Company, 304th Sanitary Train, another component of the 79th Division in which Marylanders served, operated this forward divisional dressing station at a former German clubhouse near Étraye in the Bois de la Grande Montagne. This area was the scene of heavy fighting for both the 29th and 79th Divisions in the war's final weeks. The ambulances are Ford M1917s, based on the Model T. (NARA.)

Another unit with a large contingent of Marylanders (about one third) was the 351st Field Artillery Regiment, 92nd Division, organized at Camp Meade in November 1917. A 155-millimeter regiment, it served during the Meuse-Argonne Offensive beginning on October 30 and began offensive operations on November 3, 1918. This is Battery B, firing smaller "French 75s" during maneuvers shortly after the Armistice. (NARA.)

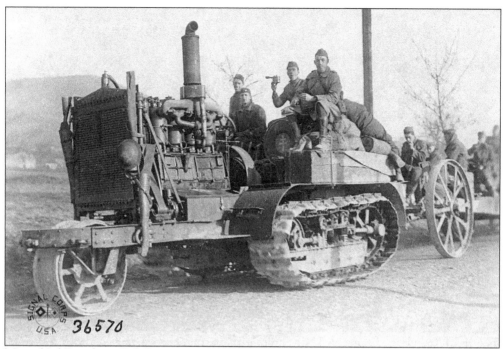

Men of 3rd Battalion, 58th Regiment, Coast Artillery Corps, haul an 8-inch howitzer of Battery E using a Holt 120-horsepower tractor near Meurthe-et-Moselle. The 3rd Battalion's Batteries E and F were organized at Fort Howard, the former mostly comprised of personnel from the Coast Defense of Baltimore (over one fourth being Marylanders), the latter from the Maryland National Guard Coast Artillery. Their weapon (below, at center) was the 8-inch howitzer M1917, an American-built version of the British Vickers BL 8-inch Mark VI, with a range of over six miles. They entered combat on November 1, 1918, in the vicinity of Jezainville, south of German-held Metz. (Both, NARA.)

This photograph of officers' mess cooks at Aubreville on November 10, 1918, is one of only a handful ever taken of the 808th Pioneer Infantry, which formed at Camp Meade with a sizable contingent of Marylanders (about one sixth) and served during the Meuse-Argonne Offensive. The predominantly African American Pioneer Infantry typically worked as laborers, building roads and rail lines and maintaining supply and munitions depots. (Courtesy of the Wisconsin Historical Society, WHS-54239.)

Another unit whose activities seem to have escaped wartime photographers was the 811th Pioneer Infantry. A rare exception was this off-duty singing quartet, performing at Saint-Nazaire after the Armistice. Over a third of the 811th, which served at docks and depots at various French ports, were Marylanders. The regiment arrived in France on November 4, 1918, and returned during June and July 1919. (Courtesy of the Harry S. Truman Library and Museum.)

Fallen soldiers of the 79th Division are buried in a temporary cemetery near the battered Bois de Consenvoye on November 8, 1918. Although the 313th Infantry mostly remained in reserve during the war's final days, it nonetheless lost 48 killed and 232 wounded from November 3 to 11. Its wartime casualty rate totaled 39 percent. The 79th was named the "Cross of Lorraine" Division, commemorating its role in liberating the region. (NARA.)

As Germany collapsed both politically and militarily, Kaiser Wilhelm II abdicated on November 9, 1918. On November 11, soldiers received word that an armistice would take effect at 11:00 a.m. Many American commanders, eager for glory, continued pressing forward under fire until that deadline. Here, soldiers of Company H, 313th Infantry, stand by the imposing yet now surreally benign German-fortified Hill 356 northeast of Gibercy on November 13. (NARA.)

Seven

MARYLANDERS "OVER THERE"

Sgt. Henry Gunther was hounded for his German heritage, particularly after superiors caught him disparaging the war. The Baltimorean exhibited tremendous bravery and, stung by a demotion to private, became increasingly reckless in combat. Gunther posthumously received the Distinguished Service Cross for single-handedly charging a German machine gun position during the war's final moments on November 11, 1918. He was the last soldier killed on the western front. (Author's collection.)

Like many units, Company C, 115th Infantry, took a panoramic group photograph before departing for France. Twelve never returned: Pvt. Frank Bartoszewicz, Pfc. James Doubek, Pfc. George Doxzon, Cpl. Charles Harrer, Pvt. Maks Holka, Pvt. James Stitz, and Pfc. Henry Zahner of

First Lt. William Watters of Howard County, drafted as a private, completed officer training at Camp Meade and was commissioned in June 1918. During the Meuse-Argonne Offensive, he led a platoon of Company B, 313th Infantry. He was killed near Madeleine Farm on September 29, 1918, during an assault against the Kreimhilde Stellung ordered "regardless of cost." He is buried at Meuse-Argonne American Cemetery. (Courtesy of the Howard County Historical Society.)

Baltimore; Cpl. John Townsend of Cambridge; Bugler Joseph McCormick of Catonsville; Cpl. Henry Davis of Federalsburg; Pfc. George Thompson of Gardenville; and Sgt. John Herpel of Highlandtown. (LOC.)

Maj. German Horton Hunt Emory of Allegany County and Baltimore commanded the 3rd Battalion of the 320th Infantry, 80th Division. He was cited for gallantry on the first day of the Meuse-Argonne Offensive, leading his men against determined German resistance. Horton was killed by enemy machine gunners during an assault near Sommerance on November 1, 1918, posthumously receiving the Distinguished Service Cross for his brave leadership under fire. (Author's collection.)

Ens. Charles Hazeltine Hammann, US Naval Reserve, flew Macchi M.5 seaplanes on patrol from Naval Air Station Porto Corsini in Italy. On August 21, 1918, the Baltimorean became the first US Navy pilot to receive the Medal of Honor, for his heroic rescue of a squadron mate downed by an Austro-Hungarian pilot over the Adriatic Sea. Hammann died in a flying accident at Langley Field, Virginia, in June 1919. (NHHC.)

Pfc. Henry Gilbert Costin of Baltimore was an automatic rifleman with Company H of the 115th Infantry. Although wounded during an artillery and gas barrage shortly before the Meuse-Argonne Offensive, he soon returned to the front. Costin posthumously received the Medal of Honor for his heroic actions on October 8, 1918, helping to assault German machine gun positions near the Bois de Consenvoye even after being mortally wounded. (Author's collection.)

First Lt. George Buchanan Redwood, an intelligence officer with the 28th Infantry, 1st Division, received the Distinguished Service Cross for leading a dangerous patrol on March 28, 1918. Redwood was killed during the Battle of Cantigny two months later and was posthumously awarded a second Distinguished Service Cross for bravery under fire. Baltimore honored its first fallen officer by renaming German Street Redwood Street. (Courtesy of Harvard University Archives, HUD 3567.219.2 photograph 310.)

Pfc. George Garland Clark of Baltimore was a Maryland National Guardsman serving with the 117th Trench Mortar Battery. During the Meuse-Argonne Offensive he and other men of the 117th were detached for temporary courier duty with the 166th Infantry, 42nd Division. Clark was killed by shrapnel during a German artillery barrage near Landres-et-Saint-Georges on October 17, 1918, and is buried at Meuse-Argonne American Cemetery. (Author's collection.)

Sgt. William Butler of Salisbury was working in New York in April 1917 and served with Company L of the 369th Infantry Regiment, the famed "Harlem Hellfighters." The 369th won many honors under French command. Butler, an automatic rifleman, earned the Distinguished Service Cross and French Croix de Guerre with Palm for breaking up a German raiding party and rescuing its American prisoners on August 18, 1918. (Author's collection.)

Alfred Noble of Federalsburg graduated from St. John's College in 1917, having already served on the Mexican border. Commissioned a second lieutenant in the US Marine Corps, he earned numerous awards fighting with the 6th Marines, 2nd Division, in France, including the Distinguished Service Cross and Navy Cross. He would serve as a major general during World War II and retire as a four-star general in 1956. (Author's collection.)

Lt. Col. Millard Tydings of Havre de Grace received the Distinguished Service Cross for extraordinary heroism and a 29th Division Citation for Gallantry in Action while commanding the 111th Machine Gun Battalion during the Meuse-Argonne Offensive in October 1918. After the war, Tydings served as a state senator, congressman, and then US senator from 1927 to 1951. (Millard E. Tydings Papers, Special Collections, University of Maryland Libraries, courtesy of Sen. Joseph D. Tydings.)

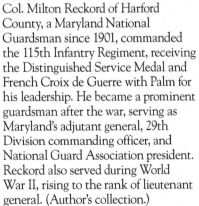

Col. Milton Reckord of Harford County, a Maryland National Guardsman since 1901, commanded the 115th Infantry Regiment, receiving the Distinguished Service Medal and French Croix de Guerre with Palm for his leadership. He became a prominent guardsman after the war, serving as Maryland's adjutant general, 29th Division commanding officer, and National Guard Association president. Reckord also served during World War II, rising to the rank of lieutenant general. (Author's collection.)

Lt. Comdr. William Howard Michael of Perryman was a Navy surgeon with the 6th Marines in France. He earned the Distinguished Service Cross (shown being presented by General Pershing) and Navy Cross for his actions during the Battle of Belleau Wood on June 6, 1918, operating a dressing station for wounded Marines under direct enemy fire. He later served with Johns Hopkins Hospital's Base Hospital 18. (NARA.)

Lt. Col. Robert Joshua Gill of Baltimore received the French Croix de Guerre with Palm while commanding the 117th Trench Mortar Battery for repulsing a German tank and infantry attack on July 5, 1918. In September 1918, he became assistant chief of staff of the 42nd Division under Douglas MacArthur. Gill also served during World War II and at the Nuremberg Trials, reaching the rank of brigadier general. (Author's collection.)

On July 31, 1918, Sgt. John H.E. Hoppe of Baltimore (left) and Pfc. Andy Youngbar of Fairfield, Company K, 115th Infantry, endured a predawn German raid on their newly occupied outpost near Gildwiller, Alsace. Despite serious grenade wounds, the two men aggressively counterattacked against the superior force and continued engaging despite receiving additional wounds. For their bravery in turning back the enemy assault, both received the Distinguished Service Cross and French Croix de Guerre with Silver Star. They were later medically evacuated to the United States. Hoppe was a prewar National Guardsman. Youngbar was one of three brothers in the service and the only one to serve overseas; his older brother, James, died of influenza at Camp Meade. (NARA.)

Capt. Francis Warrington Gillet of Baltimore served in Britain's Royal Air Force in 1918 after the US Army refused him flight training. He became America's second highest-scoring ace, with 20 confirmed victories flying Sopwith Dolphins with No. 79 Squadron. He was twice awarded the Distinguished Flying Cross. (Courtesy of the Ola Sater Collection, History of Aviation Collection, Special Collections and Archives Division, Eugene McDermott Library, The University of Texas at Dallas.)

Lt. Comdr. Edward McDonnell of Baltimore received the Medal of Honor for actions during the Battle of Veracruz, Mexico, in April 1914. During World War I, he served as a naval aviator with the Northern Bombing Group in France and Italy, earning the Navy Cross for heroic leadership. He retired as a vice admiral in 1951. McDonnell was killed in the bombing of National Airlines Flight 2511 in 1960. (NARA.)

Maj. William Preston Lane Jr. of Hagerstown served as the 115th Infantry's regimental adjutant. He received a 29th Division Citation for Gallantry in Action for guiding ambulances and wounded men from the front while under fire near the Bois de Consenvoye on October 8–9, 1918. Lane served as a lieutenant colonel during World War II and was Maryland's 31st attorney general and 52nd governor. (Courtesy of the Goddard family.)

Pfc. Daniel Nelson of Baltimore served with Maryland's 1st Separate Company and later Company I, 372nd Infantry. He arrived in France in April 1918, seeing combat during Germany's Champagne-Marne Offensive. Nelson was wounded on September 29, 1918, during the Meuse-Argonne Offensive, and eventually medically evacuated to the United States. He brought back Kaiser Bill, his "liberated" German companion. Nelson was discharged as a disabled veteran in June 1919. (NARA.)

Sgt. Rufus Pinckney of Baltimore served with Maryland's 1st Separate Company, and then Headquarters Company, 372nd Infantry. On August 16, 1918, he received the French Croix de Guerre with Bronze Star for rescuing a French comrade during a heavy bombardment near Montzéville. Pinckney was later wounded during the Meuse-Argonne Offensive on September 30, 1918. He served with distinction as a Pittsburgh police officer after the war. (Author's collection.)

First Sgt. Carl Michael of Baltimore, a member of the 117th Trench Mortar Battery, left college to serve in France. He received a 42nd Division Citation for Gallantry in Action for his leadership on March 9, 1918, supporting American infantry despite heavy German artillery fire. He received an officer's commission in October 1918, finishing the war as a first lieutenant. Note the trench mortar insignia on his sleeve. (Author's collection.)

Baltimore Orioles first baseman Jack Bentley of Sandy Spring, shown playing for the Washington Senators in 1916, was drafted in 1917. He declined a religious exemption despite being a Quaker and rose to the rank of lieutenant in the 313th Infantry Regiment. During the Meuse-Argonne Offensive, he commanded the regimental sapper pioneer platoon, cutting barbed wire and clearing the path of the main assault force. (LOC.)

Second Lt. George Spencer Barnes of Talbot County was a dental surgeon, a profession in high demand as the Army expanded due to the numerous anticipated facial wounds. Drafted and assigned to officer training at Camp Funston, Kansas, he served with the 349th Machine Gun Battalion, 92nd "Buffalo Soldiers" Division, the only African American division to see combat as a unit. (Courtesy of the Kenneth Spencer Research Library, University of Kansas Libraries.)

Pfc. James M. Cain of Annapolis and Chestertown, a *Baltimore Sun* journalist, served with the 79th Division's Headquarters Troop. During the Meuse-Argonne Offensive, he performed hazardous duty as a runner for Maj. Gen. Joseph Kuhn. Cain gained fame as a crime novelist after the war, best known for the noir classic *The Postman Always Rings Twice*. (LOC.)

Nurse Vashti Bartlett of Montgomery County and Baltimore served with the American Red Cross in France and Belgium before America entered the war. She later joined the US Army Nursing Corps, returning to France in 1918 as chief nurse of Base Hospital 71. After the Armistice, she served with the Red Cross in Vladivostok, Russia, aiding refugees and supporting the American Expeditionary Force Siberia during the Russian Civil War. (NARA.)

Eight

VICTORY AND
REMEMBRANCE

Men of the 110th Field Artillery Regiment, 29th Division, greet loved ones during a brief stop on May 28, 1919. Their train was en route from Camp Stuart, Virginia, to Camp Meade for demobilization. The 110th, whose 2nd Battalion was comprised of Maryland National Guardsmen, had been moving to the front when the Armistice was declared. Despite seeing no combat, 15 men of the regiment did not return. (NARA.)

The exuberant Armistice Day celebrations that swept Baltimore on November 11, 1918, were captured from the *Baltimore Sun*'s building at Charles and Baltimore Streets. Crowds began forming early in the morning as news broke that the Armistice had finally gone into effect at 11:00 a.m. local time on the western front—the 11th hour of the 11th day of the 11th month. They continued surging past midnight, with the *Baltimore American* reporting a half-million people in the streets. Saloons and other businesses closed early, with the state and city governments declaring a general holiday. The *Sun* called it "the greatest day in the history of the world" in its issue of November 12, in which these photographs were published. Armistice Day was marked each year thereafter, becoming a national holiday in 1938. In 1954, it was changed to Veterans Day, honoring all military veterans. Armistice Day is observed concurrently with Remembrance Day in many of the former Allied powers. (Author's collection.)

Gen. John J. Pershing wrote in AEF General Order No. 203 on November 12, 1918: "The enemy has capitulated. It is fitting that I address myself in thanks directly to the officers and soldiers of the American Expeditionary Forces who by their heroic efforts have made possible this glorious result. Our armies, hurriedly raised and hastily trained, met a veteran enemy, and by courage, discipline and skill always defeated him. Without complaint you have endured incessant toil, privation and danger. You have seen many of your comrades make the supreme sacrifice that freedom may live. I thank you for the patience and courage with which you have endured. I congratulate you upon the splendid fruits of victory which your heroism and the blood of our gallant dead are now presenting to our nation. Your deeds will live forever on the most glorious pages of America's history." (Author's collection.)

Elements of the 351st Field Artillery, including 1st Battalion, arrive in Hoboken aboard the transport USS *Louisville* on February 16, 1919, ten days after leaving France. The 1st Battalion was primarily from the Pittsburgh area but still included many Marylanders. Marylanders of the 2nd Battalion arrived in Philadelphia aboard the liner SS *Northland* on February 21. The 351st completed demobilization at Camp Meade on March 7. (NARA.)

Men of the 115th Infantry and 112th Machine Gun Battalion (the latter 30 percent Marylanders) crowd the deck of the USS *Artemis* as it enters Newport News, Virginia, on May 24, 1919. After being greeted by Maryland governor Emerson Harrington, they marched to nearby Camp Stuart, where they received a homecoming welcome from the Maryland Home Kitchen, run by volunteers serving crab, fried chicken, strawberries, ice cream, and other favorites. (Author's collection.)

Men of Headquarters Company, 313th Infantry Regiment, pose at Newport News after disembarking from the transport USS *Antigone* on May 29, 1919. After marching to Camp Stuart, they too were welcomed by the Maryland Home Kitchen, newly staffed by women of the 313th Auxiliary. They then rushed back to Baltimore for the state's homecoming celebration. Two battalions of the 313th aboard the delayed USS *Paysandu* missed the festivities. (Author's collection.)

Men of the 115th Infantry Regiment parade triumphantly through Baltimore during festivities to honor Maryland's fighting men on May 31, 1919. They are shown making their way west down Baltimore Street on a circuitous route that ended at the 5th Regiment Armory. The photograph appears to have been taken from the Baltimore Bargain House (now the Nancy S. Grasmick Building), at the corner of Baltimore and Liberty Streets. (Author's collection.)

The 808th Pioneer Infantry parades past Baltimore City Hall down Holliday Street on June 25, 1919. In few meaningful ways were Maryland's African American veterans treated as equals to their white comrades-in-arms, but the 808th's triumphant homecoming, warmly welcomed by a multiracial crowd, might have been cause for optimism. Unfortunately, the goodwill on display that day contrasted sharply with the overall treatment of returning African American veterans. The "Red Summer" of 1919, a wave of deadly anti-black violence that swept across the southern and central United States as the military demobilized, was already underway. Many of its victims were veterans, some targeted for being in uniform or wearing their medals as they returned home. In just over three weeks, soldiers from Camp Meade would be sent to quell a major race riot in Washington, DC, instigated by white servicemen. Returning African American veterans, who had fought Germany to "make the world safe for democracy," would help lay the foundations of the civil rights movement. (Courtesy of the Baltimore City Planning Commission.)

Maryland's War Memorial was dedicated in April 1925, consisting of a building and plaza prominently situated facing Baltimore City Hall. Baltimorean Lawrence Hall Fowler was the memorial's architect, having won a 1921 design competition. French marshal Ferdinand Foch, wartime commander-in-chief of the Allied armies, came to Baltimore to participate in the groundbreaking ceremony. The elaborate building contains plaques with the names of all Marylanders who died during their wartime service, as well as an auditorium and assembly room for use by veterans' and civic organizations. Since 1977, it has also officially memorialized Marylanders who gave the ultimate sacrifice in World War II, the Korean War, and the Vietnam War. Among the groups that it frequently hosts is the East Coast Branch (USA) of the Western Front Association, an organization dedicated to promoting interest in the history of the First World War. (Courtesy of the Maryland Historical Society.)

First Lt. Merrill Rosenfeld, a well-known Baltimore attorney, was a veteran Maryland National Guardsman who served with Company G, 115th Infantry. Rosenfeld was killed assaulting a machine gun position during the Meuse-Argonne Offensive, posthumously receiving the Distinguished Service Cross for heroism. His grieving father, Israel, bequeathed funds for the Grove of Remembrance Pavilion in Druid Hill Park in his memory. The Grove of Remembrance, located just to the left of the Maryland Zoo's main entrance, was originally planted in 1919 to honor the war dead of each state and the city of Baltimore, the Allied powers, and President Wilson. Trees were later added to honor veterans of World War II and Korea, the new states of Alaska and Hawaii, General Pershing, and Pres. Dwight D. Eisenhower. Baltimorean architect Edward L. Palmer Jr. designed the pavilion, erected in 1927. (Both, author's collection.)

Throughout the decade after the war, numerous monuments and memorials were erected in towns large and small across the country, ranging from simple plaques to elaborate statues and memorial buildings. One popular genre was the doughboy monument. Lonaconing's example, dedicated in 1925, honors the town's 27 war dead. Although the United States was spared the scale of losses suffered by other belligerents, the war nonetheless had a lasting impact. (Author's collection)

Frederick's Victory Monument was dedicated on Armistice Day, 1924, the centerpiece of the new Memorial Grounds (now Memorial Park) across from the Frederick Armory. Sculpted by Giuseppe Moretti, it lists the names of all from Frederick County who served and 83 who gave their lives during the war. Brig. Gen. Milton Reckord spoke at the dedication. The park, a former graveyard, was gifted by the Evangelical Reformed Church. (Author's collection.)

Dedicated via radio by Pres. Franklin D. Roosevelt in 1937, the Montfaucon American Monument commemorates the victory at Meuse-Argonne. Over 200 feet tall, with an observation deck to view the battlefield, it towers over the ruined village through which the 313th Infantry fought on September 27, 1918. The 313th suffered a casualty rate of approximately 14 percent from September 26 to 30, with 218 killed and 742 wounded. (Courtesy of the American Battle Monuments Commission.)

The 372nd Infantry's contributions were relatively unknown in America but not forgotten in France. This postcard shows Msgr. Ernest Neveux, bishop of Arsinoe, dedicating his country's monument to the 372nd during a ceremony on October 25, 1919. The obelisk, located just southeast of Monthois, reads: "157e Division—In Memory of the Members of the 372nd U.S. Infantry Killed in Action, September 26, 1918 to October 7, 1918." (Author's collection.)

This French postcard shows the Meuse-Argonne American Cemetery as it appeared shortly after the war. At its peak, the cemetery held more than 25,000 American dead, over 10,000 of whom were eventually repatriated. Today it is administered by the American Battle Monuments Commission and is the largest American cemetery in Europe. It is the final resting place of 200 Marylanders and memorializes another 16 missing in action. (Author's collection.)

Meuse-Argonne American Cemetery is pictured as it appears today. Marylanders are also interred or memorialized at each of the other American World War I cemeteries in Europe: Suresnes, Aisne-Marne, Somme, Saint-Mihiel, Oise-Aisne, Brookwood, and Flanders Field. At least 1,529 Marylanders died of all causes during the war. (Courtesy of the American Battle Monuments Commission.)

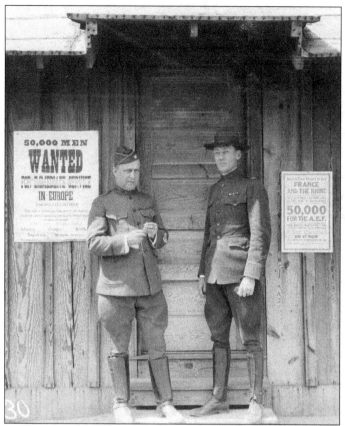

After the Armistice, Camp Meade continued to train soldiers who volunteered for occupation duty. Recruiting posters advertised good pay and a chance to see Europe. The American commitment to the Allied occupation of the Rhineland would last until January 24, 1923. The war and harsh Allied peace terms devastated Germany, where economic hardships and political unrest ultimately created the conditions in which Adolf Hitler (a World War I veteran) rose to power. Less than 20 years after the last doughboys returned home, many survivors of this "war to end all wars" would see their children off to another war in Europe, to help liberate the continent from the tyranny of Nazi Germany. (Both, NARA.)

SELECT BIBLIOGRAPHY

Bauer, William E., and John P. Judge Jr., comps. *Baltimore and the Draft: An Historical Record.* Baltimore, MD: Monumental Print Co., 1919.

Crowell, Benedict. *America's Munitions, 1917–1918.* Washington, DC: Government Printing Office, 1919.

Ferrell, Robert H. *America's Deadliest Battle: Meuse-Argonne, 1918.* Lawrence, KS: University Press of Kansas, 2007.

Maryland War Records Commission. *Maryland in the World War, 1917–1919: Military and Naval Service Records.* 3 vols. Baltimore, MD: Twentieth Century Press, 1933.

Messimer, Dwight R. *The Baltimore Sabotage Cell.* Annapolis. MD: Naval Institute Press, 2015.

Order of Battle of the United States Land Forces in the World War. 3 vols. Washington, DC: Center of Military History, 1988.

Reynolds, Frederick C., ed. *115th Infantry U.S.A. In the World War.* Baltimore, MD: The Read-Taylor Co., 1920.

Scott, Emmett J. *Scott's Official History of the American Negro in the World War.* Chicago, IL: Homewood Press, 1919.

Thorn, Henry C. Jr. *History of the 313th Infantry "Baltimore's Own."* New York, NY: Wynkoop Hallenbeck Crawford Co., 1920.

Walker, William. *Betrayal at Little Gibraltar.* New York, NY: Scribner, 2016.

In addition to the above volumes, factual material for this book was drawn from various other published unit and administrative histories; the *Baltimore Afro-American*, *Baltimore American*, *Baltimore Sun*, and other Maryland newspapers; and the following record groups at the National Archives and Records Administration in College Park, Maryland, and Washington, DC: US Navy, Bureau of Ships (RG 19), Bureau of Yards and Docks (RG 71), and Bureau of Ordnance (RG 74); Department of the Navy (RG 80); US Army, Office of the Chief Signal Officer (RG 111), American Expeditionary Forces (RG 120), and Office of the Chief of Ordnance (RG 156); and War Department General and Special Staffs (RG 165).

Visit us at
arcadiapublishing.com